Teaching Makes a Difference

Second Edition

by

Carol Cummings, Ph.D.

**with First Edition contributions
from
Cliff Nelson and Dian Shaw, Ph.D.**

Table of Contents

Instructional decisions...apart from knowledge of content, planning skills, use of materials, human relations, and classroom management skills...are those decisions a teacher can make to facilitate the **learning** of students.

Anderson & Faust

Chapter 1

Instructional Skills

Can you:
• explain the interest in instructional skills
• list the major organizers for this book
• explain each of the elements of instruction

Isn't it a relief to know that we do make a difference? In the '60's you got the impression any able-bodied individual could be pulled off the street and put into the classroom. Focus was on which textbook to use, not which teacher! "Teacher-proof" curriculum materials were stressed. The most important *agent* for instruction and student learning was ignored:

the teacher!

As late as 1977 "teachers were viewed either as weak links in the educational process to be circumvented or as technicians to be programmed" (Porter & Brophy, 1988). Not so today. We now have more than enough data to prove that

teachers make a difference!

The last twenty years have been a Renaissance period in education: a period of vigorous intellectual activity. The effect of this period has been to link teacher behavior to student achievement and provide a knowledge base for school learning (Wang et al., 1993). Researchers left their laboratories of maze-running rats and pecking pigeons to observe teachers in action! Tools were developed to describe and measure teaching in a quantitative manner. These descriptions were then related to achievement. Promising teaching strategies were isolated and taught to experimental groups of teachers, with the result that student achievement increased. While this research validated good teaching practice, it also stimulated criticism of less effective teaching practices.

"Teaching Must Be More Productive and It Can Be"

This theme, from Educational Leadership's October 1987 issue, expresses both the widespread disaffection with our educational system and a sense of optimism. First, let's explore reasons for the disaffection.

When U.S. students are compared with students of other countries on math and science knowledge, we are typically at the bottom. Even when our top students are compared with top students in other countries, the achievement gap persists (Stevenson, 1993; Stevenson, 1987).

A Nation at Risk (1983), reporting on the quality of education in America, suggested that "if an unfriendly foreign power had attempted to impose on America the mediocre educational performance that exists today, we might well have viewed it as an act of war."

It's pretty obvious that educational reform has been a high priority item for many groups. New reports regularly surface forecasting gloom and doom. Ironically, though, the move has been to restructure schools, provide site based management, or redesign program. Will all this reorganization improve classroom teaching—the most important variable we control that influences student learning?

Optimism

Our goal in this text is to view the glass as half full—not half empty. Our focus will be on what we've "added to the glass" over that last two decades, not on what's wrong. When over 300 meta-analyses and reviews were synthesized, classroom instruction and climate had nearly as much impact on learning as student aptitude (Wang, et al., 1994). Let's use this knowledge base to refine teaching practice. As you consciously take time to add precision to your teaching, you will experience success that enhances your own self-concept. Wouldn't you feel like patting yourself on the back if, at the end of your lesson, most students had mastered your objective? Wouldn't it be great to be able to analyze that lesson and know that you helped students learn because of the decisions you made?

Much of the research we'll discuss will confirm the effectiveness of skills you're already using, consciously or intuitively. By bringing intuitive skills to a conscious level, you can fine-tune your own instructional decision-making and become better able to communicate with fellow teachers. Every profession has a precise vocabulary with which to communicate. A doctor can recommend either medical or surgical "aseptic procedures" and the nurse fully comprehends. An attorney can request a "writ of habeas corpus" and a fellow attorney can produce that exact document. As we increase the precision of our instructional skill, it's not unusual to hear vocabulary such as "task analysis", "congruency", "critical attribute", and "covert involvement" around the faculty room...instead of, "If I have to tell that kid one more time...."

Check Yourself Out!

Before we give you the outline for this book—an outline of instructional skills—let's stop and have you diagnose your own conscious knowledge of instructional decision making. Read the following description of a lesson segment and see what evidence you can find of effective teacher decisions. Try to keep everything in perspective—you're looking for evidence of instructional skill. We're separating this skill from content knowledge, planning skill, human relationship skills, materials use, and classroom management.

Imagine yourself as an observer in the back of an eighth-grade classroom of thirty students. It's the first day of a new semester and the teacher has just explained to the students that they will be working on improvement of their writing skills. They're going to begin by learning the attributes of a complete sentence.

Teacher: "Today I would like to develop your understanding of the two basic parts of a sentence: the subject and the predicate. The subject will name the person, place, or thing the sentence is about. The predicate will tell what action is being done. I'll give you some examples." (Gives three examples of each.) "Now let me have you try matching some subjects with the appropriate predicate."

A worksheet with twenty sentences on it is passed out. The first few examples are:

1. The fire	a. chirped all morning.
2. Several villains	b. burns warmly.
3. Colorful robins	c. were hiding behind the rocks

Teacher: "When you finish this practice sheet, check your answers against the key provided in the back of the room."

From this brief portion of a lesson, can you identify teacher decisions that promoted learning?

What suggestions do you have that would *add* to the quality of the teacher's instructional decisions?

As you read on, match your analysis to the analysis the author provides later in this chapter.

Instructional Decision Making

Students learn more when their teacher *structures* the information within the lesson. We want to practice what we preach in this book so here is your organizer (and the way we will structure instructional decision making):

1. Select the Objective
2. Teach to the Objective
3. Monitor and Adjust
4. Use Principles of Learning
   Motivational Principles
   Principles of Retention
   Active Participation
   Mental Set
5. Plan Better Lessons

Teaching is far more complex than ever before realized (Garmston & Wellman, 1995). How easy it would be if we only had to deliver content. Instead, we must decide whether the content is at the correct level of difficulty and complexity for the learners (select the objective). We have to decide what is the most effective and efficient way to present the material (teach to the objective). We need to determine how many of our students are learning the content *while* we are teaching (monitor and adjust). We must decide how to motivate the students, keep them actively involved in the learning, and help them remember the information (use principles of learning). In Chapter 10, Plan Better Lessons, we will apply these instructional decisions to lesson planning, the first step in teaching.

Select the Objective

To illustrate what is meant by "selecting the objective near the correct level of difficulty," imagine that this paragraph is going to teach you how to spell the word "school." In fact, close your eyes and practice spelling it three times. Now, write the word several times in the space below:

Ridiculous? Why waste your time when you already know how to spell the word? The objective is too easy. Transfer your feelings to the classroom. Think about the student who is taught the food pyramid in the second, fourth, and sixth grades. Then the same student enters secondary school and has to go through the same lesson again. A better use of time would be to find out how much the student already knows about the food pyramid, and then provide instruction on the missing information.

Now imagine that we gave you a list of theorems to prove and asked you to construct at least six valid proofs. Would you be willing? For many of you this activity would be too difficult—you may not have the requisite skills and knowledge. Even if you were provided with an explanation of axioms and theorems, you might still insist that you're wasting your time. Back to the reality of the classroom. If a teacher tries to teach the Pythagorean theorem to a student who can't square numbers or who can't find the square root of a number, that instruction is a waste of time. The objective is too difficult.

Teach to the Objective

Teaching to the objective implies that if a teacher identifies a goal and keeps teacher and learner activities directed to that goal, achieving that goal is easier and more efficient in time and effort. There's a payoff for the learners, too. Imagine the following lesson:

The teacher started to teach the class the characteristics of the four seasons of the year, starting with winter. The discussion went from owls nesting in the month of February, to animal tracks in the snow, to the fact that a gasoline shortage during the winter was a possibility, to the limitation of natural resources and finally to a homework assignment requiring a list of things students could do to save energy.

If you are confused, guess how the kids felt. Very little time was spent on the objective the teacher wanted to teach—the objective the students were to be tested on later. How unfortunate for the kids. There's a direct relationship between the amount of time students spend on a learning objective and their achievement of that objective (Brophy, 1992).

Not all lessons go as far astray as the one we just described. Sometimes the mismatch between what a teacher wants to accomplish and what the teacher does to accomplish it can be as subtle as this:

Objective	Activity
The learner will visually discriminate the letter *m*	Coloring pictures beginning with *m*

Auditory discrimination is not the same skill as visual discrimination. What the students practiced did not match the objective!

Monitor and Adjust

Monitoring is really applying a system of quality control through which the teacher determines whether or not each step in the teaching-learning process was effective. Effective teaching is self-correcting; that is, we continually check student understanding to see if our instruction is working! You've probably experienced a class where the teacher failed to monitor during instruction. The author completed a statistics class where this happened. The teacher, an expert in his field, taught to his objectives the whole quarter. He rarely got off target. He carefully wrote all formulas on the board as he explained how to solve them. The problem was that he had no idea how much of this instruction made any sense to the learners until the end of the quarter when he gave a final exam. Many students were lost. By that time it was too late to make any adjustments!

Check Yourself Out!

Speaking of monitoring and adjusting, we'll need to monitor your understanding throughout this book. We'll provide questions or reviews periodically and ask you to respond. You'll have to assume the role of "teacher" when you check your answers. If your answers match, read on. If they don't, you might want to improve your understanding by reviewing the sections dealing with that topic or explore some of the references cited in that chapter.

> 1. This book will discuss
>   a. All the skills of a teacher
>   b. Classroom management skills
>   c. Instructional skills
>   d. Knowledge of content
> 2. Describe the three areas of instructional decision making discussed so far.

Did you select "c" for the first question? That's the correct answer because, remember, this book is addressing only one dimension of teaching: instructional decision making. We're going to look at four basic instructional decisions, but the three mentioned so far are, select the objective, teach to the objective, and monitor and adjust.

Use Principles of Learning

Educational psychology has contributed immensely to our understanding of how humans learn. In this book, we'll examine only a few of the principles identified by research, particularly those we can use to increase our students' motivation, help them remember information, and speed up their learning. We all use these principles in varying degree as we teach, though perhaps not consciously. By labeling them and bringing them to a conscious level, we will be better equipped to motivate the student who says, "I don't want to do it," or to plan a practice period so that every minute counts. Let's look at a few of these principles of learning theory translated into classroom practice, starting with those concerning motivation.

Haven't you, at some point, encountered a student who would rather chat with a friend than listen to you? Rather than interrupt your teaching, you tried just walking over and standing by that student while continuing what you were saying. Chances are that child terminated the private conversation to stare at you. That's an example of using the principle of level of concern to help a learner focus. If we find that that familiar strategy doesn't work to motivate the student, it will be useful to know about other principles of motivation that could work. We might be more successful with this particular student if we try the principle of interest. Suppose the lesson happened to be on the basic parts of a play, and we know that our chatty student watches a lot of television. We might then give examples from a popular TV program. Or perhaps with this student some extrinsic reward would be an effective motivator. It might take only the words: "You may choose a free-time activity when you finish your work."

These motivational principles need to be combined with principles of retention so that students may grasp and remember the lesson. Building as much <u>meaning</u> as possible into every lesson will facilitate retention. We've all heard about the importance of making lessons meaningful, but we need to identify specific strategies that increase the degree of meaningfulness. For example, pointing out a *logical relationship* increases meaning. A teacher beginning a lesson on how to write a formal business letter can hook into the previous learning students have accomplished on writing friendly letters. "The parts of this kind of letter will be similar to the parts of a friendly letter. You need to learn, though, about one additional part."

<u>Active participation</u> is a principle of learning that affects both motivation and retention as well as speed of learning. How much and how fast students learn in a lesson are dependent upon how actively involved they are in the lesson. A teacher can encourage active involvement simply through the phrasing of questions. "Everyone consider the events leading up to the French Revolution. Jot down as many as you can remember on your think pad." If we want all students to learn, then we want *all* students involved!

Check Yourself Out!

Remember that lesson segment on the two basic parts of a sentence? Ready for some feedback? Compare your analysis of that lesson to the following:

Select the objective. Having no indication as to how the teacher selected the objective, we can only ask the question: how much did the teacher know about the students' prior knowledge of the subject? Was the teacher aware of their writing skills or their understanding of the basic parts of a sentence? Did she do a diagnostic test?

10

Teach to the objective. The teacher's explanation appeared to be targeted to the objective. However, the activity the teacher selected for the students did *not* lead to the accomplishment of the objective. Matching the sentence parts was not a measure of the learner's understanding of subjects and predicates. It was only checking their comprehension of words. A better targeted activity might be to give students complete sentences and have them underline the subject once and the predicate twice.

Monitor and Adjust. There was no indication that the teacher checked to see if learning was taking place before the students were given work to do independently.

Use principles of learning. From this brief description, we can identify the use of a variable of motivation theory: immediate and specific knowledge of results. (The students could check their own work as soon as they were finished.)

How did your analysis compare? If you feel successful, you probably don't need to read the remainder of this book. However, if you feel a need for further refinement of your understanding of instructional decision making, that's what the rest of this book is all about. We won't give you a recipe for teaching. Rather, we'll help you refine your decisions to increase the probability that students will learn *"because of you, not in spite of you!"*

Good teaching is not prescriptive. Good teaching does not follow an inflexible script. Instead, good teaching involves complex decision making (1) before the lesson begins, (2) while the lesson is being taught, and (3) after the lesson is completed. Porter and Brophy (1988) describe the model for effective teaching as:

Preactive + Interactive + Self-Correcting

The instructional decision-making model will help us refine a lesson in the planning stage (preactively), during a lesson (interactively), and afterwards (self-correcting). With the lesson segment we saw on subjects and predicates, we need to be reminded that ultimately the only true measure of success of the lesson is: Did the students learn?

Summary

Teaching is so complex! It involves classroom management, long-term planning, use of materials, human relations, and knowledge of content as well as *instructional* skills. This text will explore the area of *instructional* skills: What decisions can we make to increase the probability that students will learn? The research of the past twenty years will be organized into four basic categories. These categories encompass the basic instructional decisions you must make as a teacher:

1. **Select the Objective**
2. **Teach to the Objective**
3. **Monitor and Adjust**
4. **Use Principles of Learning**

A fifth major category, **Plan Better Lessons**, is added to assist us with our preactive decisions in the first four categories. Remember, all teachers make these decisions. Our goal is to bring them to a conscious level and increase their precision.

A child miseducated is a child lost.
J.F. Kennedy

12

Chapter 2

Select the Objective: Level of Difficulty

Can you:
• explain the steps in task analysis
• describe the use of task analysis in diagnosis

We have to start instruction somewhere. The big decision is WHERE! If we make a choice that is either too easy or too difficult for the learners we are wasting our time and theirs. We need to diagnose our students' current knowledge and skills before we can determine their instructional needs. After all,

We teach *children*, not subjects!

Ways We Commonly Diagnose

Diagnosis occurs in a variety of ways. Referring to previous records is easiest for teachers. Some districts have a record-keeping system that carefully identifies where each learner is in a sequence of incremental learnings. They have established performance objectives on which promotion is based. Each performance objective is accompanied by a rubric (i.e., a 4-point scale) to address whether the performance is insufficient, minimal, acceptable or exemplary.

Another tool is simply a profile that is kept on each student at each grade level. Diagnosis of what skills the learner has and where to begin instruction is thus far more precise than "this student has passed the sixth grade."

GRADE SIX	Mastered at:	100%	90%	80%	Date
Add mix. #'s: unlike denominator					
Sub. mix. #'s: unlike denominator					
Multiplication of fractions					
Division of fractions					
Place value: decimals					
Reading decimals					
Writing decimals					
Addition of decimals					
Subtraction of decimals					
Multiplication of decimals					
Division of dec. by whole #					
Division of decimal by dec.					

Many teachers at the secondary level use an "intuitive" diagnosis to select an objective near the correct level of difficulty. For example, the chemistry teacher, knowing that students are in their *first* chemistry class, will probably begin instruction with the easiest of chemistry objectives (chemical materials, classification of chemical elements, etc.). It's not necessary to do a formal diagnosis or refer to cumulative record cards.

Not all teachers have the luxury of cumulative records or an accurate intuitive diagnosis. Instead, they must spend time formally diagnosing their class to find out where old learning leaves off and new should begin.

Selecting the Objective Using a Task Analysis

Task analysis can add precision to any diagnosis and with it a teacher can zero in on the specific learning needs of a student. Task analysis can be invaluable in helping the teacher select an objective near the CORRECT LEVEL OF DIFFICULTY.

The process for selecting an appropriate instructional objective incorporating a task analysis can be broken down into these steps:

1. Identify a long-range objective
2. Do a task analysis
3. Design a simple diagnostic "test"
4. Give the test in order to determine which sublearnings are known/not known
5. Select the sublearning (or sub-objective) that needs to be taught

Let's take a closer look at each of these steps:

Identify a Long-Range Objective
The district curriculum guide may help you identify your long-range objective. For example, the fourth grade guide may recommend teaching long division, or the course outline for a secondary health course may recommend a unit on substance abuse. The critical thing to remember, though, is to narrow the content down. Some examples:

be able to write a paragraph	is better than	improve writing skills
list the steps of long division	is better than	able to do math problems
can discriminate fact from opinion	is better than	has critical reading skills

(Chapter 3 will have more information on *how* to write behavioral objectives.)

Do a Task Analysis
Task analysis is a description of the subskills or enabling learnings that are necessary for a student to accomplish a given objective. It's a blueprint of expected learning (not a lesson plan).
Task analysis is not a new skill for you. You've done it many times, but you may not have labeled what you were doing as task analysis! For example, near the end of the school year, you've probably done

a mental checklist of the things that needed to be accomplished before you could lock the classroom door for the summer. Let's see... student record cards need to be filled out, textbooks returned to the storeroom, supplies returned to the stockroom, desks cleaned, and so on. You described the tasks that would enable you to accomplish your objective. This same process can be followed with student learning objectives. To do a task analysis of an objective:

1. List all the sub-learnings, including
   •prerequisite skills (skills students should already know)
   •component skills (subskills in the new objective)

2. Eliminate any learnings that are not essential

3. Sequence the learnings

Listing all of the subskills involved in the objective is the toughest part of task analysis. If you leave a gap (leave out an important step), students may have trouble mastering the objective. Some suggestions that might help:

If the objective involves a product (book report, business letter, etc.), ask yourself what that product would have to look like to deserve an "A" grade. Say you were about to grade a student on the ability to write a business letter. You would probably be looking for a student who can:

Properly place the letter on a sheet of paper
Include the inside address
Include the salutation
Include the body of the letter
Paragraph properly
Include the complimentary closing

Include the name of the sender
Print (or write) neatly

If the objective involves a psychomotor skill or a math process, walk through the process yourself and label each step. Serving a tennis ball, operating a band saw, or solving division problems with decimals are examples.
When the objective is to develop a concept (democracy, simile, plot), brainstorm all of the distinctive features that describe that concept. (More about this in the chapter on concept development.)
Some objectives, especially in math, have an implied "easy to difficult" sequence in terms of types of problems. In listing the steps, try to think of as many different kinds of problems as possible, each having a new step. For example, if the long-range objective is to subtract four digits from four digits, across zeroes, you have first to establish an "anchor" (a starting place), then build one step at a time.

24	247	2476	247	2476	476
-8	-8	-8	-28	-28	-128

Notice that this is just the beginning of the task analysis. The "anchor" was established (subtract one digit from two with regrouping only in the ones place); by the sixth step we still haven't introduced zeroes or even four digits from four!
In doing a task analysis, it helps to know that there is no "ONE" task analysis for any given objective. The size of the steps is determined by the learners in your classroom. A special education teacher might identify 50 steps for the skill of tooth brushing, while a kindergarten teacher lists a dozen or so. Actually, you'll never know how good your task analysis is until you see if it works with students!
Now that you have listed the substeps to your long-range objective and eliminated any unnecessary

substeps, you should order the list. Examine it to see if substeps are dependent or independent of each other. In writing a paragraph, the ability to write a complete sentence precedes the ability to write a topic sentence or supporting sentence. The sequence is dependent. Some objectives, however, have substeps that are independent of one another. In teaching the concept of cultural diversity, it doesn't matter whether you teach about the differences in religion before or after the differences in language. The value of having the steps in your task analysis in sequential order, if there is one, will become clear when we discuss the uses of task analysis.

On the following pages are some examples of task analyses of long-range objectives.

Given the title, author, or subject, the learner will locate any book in the library.

1. CTL (Can the learner) identify and locate main areas of a library?
2. CTL locate a fiction book, given the title and the author's last name?
3. CTL locate a nonfiction book by using the Dewey Decimal Classification system?
4. CTL use the card catalog to locate a specific title or subject?

Given reference books in the library, the learner will locate specific facts or statistics.

1. CTL use the card catalog?
2. CTL use the Reader's Guide to Periodical Literature?
3. CTL locate general reference books?
4. CTL use the vertical file?

Given a paragraph containing unknown words, the learner will be able to define the unknown word in writing and underline the clues from the context of the paragraph.

1. CTL explain "context clues"?
2. CTL explain different types of contextual analysis clues?

       direct explanation clue
       experience clue
       mood or tone clue
       explanation through example
       summary clue
       synonym or restatement clue
       comparison or contrast clue
       familiar expression
       words in a series clue
       inference clue

Task analysis applies to the teaching of thinking skills and social skills as well as specific subject matter.

During a class discussion, the learner will use effective group discussion skills.

1. DTL (does the learner) speak at appropriate times?
2. DTL avoid irrelevant comments?
3. DTL contribute relevant ideas?
4. DTL speak clearly?
5. DTL speak at an appropriate rate?
6. DTL maintain eye contact with the group?
7. DTL listen attentively to others?
8. DTL paraphrase comments of other speakers?
9. DTL avoid inappropriate gestures and/or posture?
10. DTL follow directions of leader or teacher?

Given a specific problem, the learner will apply the steps in the problem solving process.

1. CTL define the problem specifically?
2. CTL list possible solutions to the problem?
3. CTL list advantages of each solution?
4. CTL list the disadvantages of each solution?
5. CTL select one of the solutions?
6. CTL implement the solution?
7. CTL choose another solution if necessary?

The learner will be able to disagree in an appropriate way.

1. DTL use eye contact?
2. DTL use a calm voice?
3. DTL express empathy for the other point of view?
4. DTL state his disagreement specifically?
5. DTL explain the reason?
6. DTL thank the person for listening?

Check Yourself Out!

This chapter is considering how we can select an objective near the correct level of difficulty. A tool that is useful in this process is a _____ of a long range objective.

To analyze the substeps or tasks leading to an objective you first
   a.
 then you
   b.
 and finally you
   c.

(Did you fill in "task analysis" on the line? Then you should have:
a. list all the sub-learnings
b. eliminate any learnings that are not essential and
c. sequence the learnings.)

So far in this process of selecting an objective, you have
   the long range objective, and
   a task analysis
Now you need to

Design and Give a <u>Simple</u> Diagnostic Test

It's necessary to determine which sublearnings are known and which ones remain to be taught. The emphasis here is on *simple* ("quick and dirty"). Spending too much time diagnosing learners will leave little time for instruction! If the long-range objective is to be able to write a paragraph, ask your students to select a topic and write a paragraph about it. Read the paragraphs using a quick coding system to keep track of the sublearnings on which students will need work.

Why not keep a supply of charts with a list of student names going down the side and the grid across the page? When diagnosing the needs of the class, simply jot down the steps you have identified across the top of the grid and you are ready to record the results of their diagnosis! A "+" in the box indicates the skill is in place; a "-" indicates it needs teaching. (See model on p. 25.) When you test students a second time to check mastery, you hope to turn the "-" into a "+".

One teacher wrote a task analysis of verb forms. He wrote a sentence for each type of verb and had his list of twenty sentences on the overhead projector when his students got to class. The class was asked to number a paper from 1 to 20 and write the verb(s) in each sentence. Ten minutes later the teacher circled the verbs on the overhead and had students correct their work. Students were then asked by a show of hands which verbs they could identify. When the hands started dropping, it was possible to pinpoint where most of the class was in terms of verb recognition.

Test yourself. Design a quick way you could diagnose a student (or class) for the learning "able to locate any book in the library." (See the task analysis for this objective on page 18.)

There are many ways to diagnose this skill. Examples might be:

> • Write the four sublearnings as questions (i.e., What would you do to find a fiction book in the library if you had the author's name?). Then you could ask students to get in pairs and "talk through" the answers to the questions while you walk around and listen.
> • Ask students to jot down what they know on a piece of paper.
> • Pass out the names of fiction and nonfiction books. Go to the library and ask students to find the books while you diagnose their skills in locating books.

(You certainly wouldn't try this option with a group of thirty students!)

Once you have determined what sublearnings are known and not known, you are ready to . . .

Select the Sublearnings to Teach

The learnings identified would be *near* the correct level of difficulty for most of the class.

To guide your practice (one more time) on the steps in selecting an objective near the correct level of difficulty, read the following example. See if you can match the teacher behaviors with steps we've discussed.

1. Identify a long-range objective.
2. Do a task analysis.
3. Design a simple diagnostic test.
4. Give the test.
5. Select the sublearnings that need to be taught.

Example:

Mr. Thomas is about to begin working on subtraction of fractions in math. Where should he start instruction so that it is neither too easy nor too difficult for his students? He could make an assumption that his students know how to subtract fractions with like denominators because that was an objective for the previous grade. But how much do they remember? Can they subtract with unlike denominators? Can they subtract mixed numbers? He decides he needs to break down this learning. He breaks it down into these sublearnings:

-subtract fractions with like denominators
-subtract mixed numbers with like denominators
-subtract fraction from a whole number
-subtract mixed number from a whole number
-subtract fractions with unlike denominators
-subtract mixed numbers with unlike denominators
    without regrouping to whole number
    with regrouping to whole number

After he identifies about eight different types of problems, all involving the subtraction of fractions, he decides to make up a small quiz. The quiz just samples a few of the kinds of problems, from the easiest to the most difficult. It looks like this:

Diagnostic Quiz
Subtraction of Fractions

7/9	3/5	5	8
-2/9	-1/5	-3 2/9	-6 7/8

7/9	3/4	5 1/3	2 1/2
-1/3	-2/3	-3 7/9	-1 4/5

After explaining to the class that he needs to find out how much they already know about subtracting fractions, Mr. Thomas gives the class about fifteen minutes to try the problems. The pretest is corrected in class. Mr. Thomas then fills out a pretest summary showing which component skills the class needs work on.

	common denom.	mixed #/ whole	unlike denom.	mixed #/ unlike den.
Mikel	+	-	-	-
Karla	+	-	-	-
Betty	+	-	-	-
Tim	-	-	-	-
Jason	+	+	+	-
Yuan	+	+	-	-

The survey shows that most students can subtract fractions with like denominators, but need help with other kinds of problems. Mr. Thomas decides his first lesson on subtraction of fractions will begin with how to subtract a mixed number from a whole number. In a very short time, the needs of the class have been diagnosed and the teacher is able to provide instruction near the correct level of difficulty.

Now, if you were matching the steps in selecting an objective near the correct level of difficulty with the above example, your results may have looked like this:

1. Select long-range objective
    subtraction of fractions
2. Do a task analysis
    the steps were listed
3. Design a simple diagnostic "test"
    samples of four different kinds of problems (steps) were put on a worksheet
4. Give the test; identify what's known, unknown
    kids took test
5. Select objective to teach (from sub-learnings)
    Mr. Thomas knew he could begin instruction with subtracting a mixed number from a whole number

To Do or Not To Do a Task Analysis

Yes, task analysis is a lot of work! But it's an invaluable tool to help us *teach children not subjects.* The evidence in support of task analysis is compelling:

• "To learn efficiently, students must be engaged in activities that are appropriate in difficulty and otherwise suited to their current achievement levels and needs" (Brophy & Good, 1986).

• To provide more success for students, we can teach in small incremental steps. Because more than 2/3 of our academic courses in schools are sequential, containing dependent substeps, we need to identify prerequisite learnings. Enhancing prerequisite learnings increases achievement (Bloom, 1984).

Task analysis isn't new. In World War II, psychologists were asked by the military to improve the training of personnel. They took "macro performance" and broke it down into "micro" behavior components. Skills such as how to assemble and disassemble an M-I rifle were analyzed and taught in a far more efficient way. Many school districts have followed suit by analyzing basic skill objectives and providing diagnostic quizzes for teachers. But, like many materials sent out of the central office, these task analyses are likely to be filed away and seldom used.

What is the solution? Make task analysis part of your thinking. Before beginning any new objective, *think*: What do my students need to know before I begin? What are the building blocks that will lead to mastery? Then you can give your students a "quick and dirty" diagnostic quiz and they will be on their way to a successful learning experience!

Summary

In this chapter, we took a long range objective and broke it down into fundamental subskills. We included both prerequisite skills and component skills. Then we used the task analysis diagnostically to find out which skills were indeed in place and which ones we'll need to teach.

The best way to eat an elephant
is to cut it into little pieces!
Henry Ford

Select the Objective: Level of Complexity

Can you:
- **give examples of the levels of Bloom's Taxonomy**
- **give a rationale for selecting higher-level objectives**
- **write a clearly defined performance objective**

You've considered selecting the content to be learned near the correct level of difficulty in Chapter Two. Finding where the learner is on that continuum of incremental learnings is only the first step. The teacher must also determine the appropriate level of complexity for the chosen objective.*

Once the teacher has made decisions as to the content and level of complexity, a decision must be made as to what the behavior of the learner should be to accomplish the objective. Voila! Now you have a performance objective!

---

*We're only going to deal with objectives for cognitive tasks. Learning objectives also include those dealing with attitudes, values, and appreciation as well as those dealing with skills necessary to play tennis, sew, or tune a car engine. We would recommend the Taxonomy of Educational Objectives Handbook II: Affective Domain (Krathwohl, Bloom, and Masia) and A Taxonomy of the Psychomotor Domain (Harrow) for a discussion of objectives in these other domains.

Before launching into a discussion of these decisions, we'd like to
-consider the need for complex thinking in schools
-explain a system for categorizing the different cognitive levels (Bloom's Taxonomy)
-give you a chance to practice thinking at each of the levels
THEN
-give you practice in clearly defining your behavioral objectives

The Need for More Complex Thinking

Our educational system is the only social institution that has the development of cognition as its primary purpose. Teachers have been the target of criticism for not doing the job. Critics are accusing us of delinquency in this very area. Is there proof of this? Unfortunately, the answer is yes.

We mentioned the *Nation at Risk* report in the first chapter. You'd think that with statements like "We have, in effect, been committing an act of unthinking, unilateral educational disarmament," we would find dramatic changes in education. Not so: in 1989, another discouraging report card was issued by the Federal Government: "American education is stagnating or deteriorating on nearly every measure in a new comparison of school performance across the country." Not only have test scores been low for decades, but on comparisons in math and science our students continue to rank near the bottom in comparisons with other nations (Stedman, 1995).

Now it's easy to be defensive, countering the criticism with excuses like changes in schools (desegregation, more electives, less homework, lower expectations) and changes in society (working mothers, absent fathers, economics, television, permissiveness). Let's put these factors aside for a moment and take a closer look at the trend in test scores. It seems that students are having the most difficulty with problems requiring *higher levels of thinking.* Try the following problems, taken from the S.A.T.:

1.Choose the word or phrase that is most nearly opposite in meaning to the word in capital letters: RECTITUDE: (a) deliberation (b) laziness (c) prejudice (d) laxity of morals (e) weakness of intellect

2. Select the lettered pair that best expresses a relationship similar to that expressed in the original pair. BALLAST: STABILITY (a) menu:appetite (b) buoy: steering (c) spice: flavor (d) grade:education (e) eclipse: clarity

3. The figure below represents a network of one-way traffic lanes. If the traffic divides equally at intersections where there are alternative directions, and in one hour 512 cars enter the traffic pattern at point B, how many cars will leave via Y?

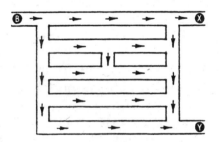

(a) 128 (b) 192 (c) 256 (d) 320 (e) 384

How do you think you did? Of the students who scored at the median on the S.A.T. as a whole, only 23% gave the correct answer for the first problem, 39% for the second, and 22% for the third. The correct answers are 1. d 2. c 3. e

Now take a second look at these problems. Ask yourself, what kind of mental gymnastics were involved in trying to solve them? Could you have relied on pure recall of information to answer them?

Probably not. In each problem you probably felt yourself involved in a careful logical analysis of the information in the problem as well as your own backlog of information. The question we need to ask ourselves is whether or not we are giving our students practice with this kind of thinking, which requires them to compare or relate and make an inductive or deductive leap on their own. Benjamin Bloom (1984) found that over 95% of the test questions our students encounter require them to think only at the lowest possible level...dealing with information.

Recommendations for improvement have invariably included the need to raise our standards. The National Council of Teachers of Mathematics (1991) recommends that solving non-routine problems in a meaningful context be a focus for the '90s. The Nation at Risk's first recommendation called for a strengthening of graduation requirements. "The teaching of English in high school should equip graduates to...comprehend, interpret, evaluate, and use what they read...." Clearly, our mandate is to extend student thinking!

Bloom's Taxonomy of the Cognitive Domain

Let's assume that we're going to make the commitment to give our students practice with extended thinking skills. Where do we begin? Perhaps the best tool a teacher can use is a classification system of the cognitive domain designed by Benjamin Bloom (1956). An understanding of these levels and the student behaviors associated with each enables a teacher to plan consciously for extended thinking activities in the classroom. More important, if the teacher is aware of the various levels of cognition, it is easier to define the objective for any given lesson—the content to be taught and the level of cognitive involvement. For example, does the student have to *use* the rules for forming plurals correctly or should the student only *recall* the rules?

We have two compelling reasons to study Bloom's Taxonomy:

...so that school is a place where real learning goes on and not just regurgitation of words

...so that we can clearly define where we're going (and we'll know what it should look like when we get there!)

What did Bloom do? He looked at the possible cognitive objectives we might teach and classified them into six categories:

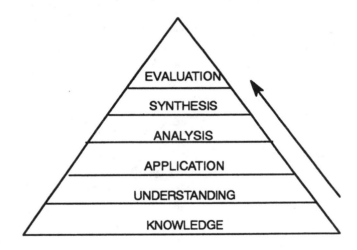

Knowledge

Excessive classroom time is devoted to the lowest level--that of having knowledge. This involves remembering previously learned material or recalling facts. Classroom examples include:

Recall the date of the Civil War.
List the steps in long division.
Name the 206 bones of the human skeleton.

Understanding   (Comprehension)

This level requires that students comprehend the facts, not just recall them. Evidence of comprehension is the explaining or summarizing of information in your own words, the translation of information to a different form of communication, or the prediction of outcomes and effects. Classroom examples include:

After reading about population growth, draw a
graph to illustrate it.
Make an outline of the story you read.
Paraphrase the Gettysburg Address.

Application

The first two levels, knowledge and understanding, represent the foundation for all higher levels of thinking. They call for primarily *convergent* thinking. Beginning with application on through the remaining levels, the student is asked to manipulate mentally the bits of information previously learned and create an answer. This kind of thinking is often called *divergent*.

At the level of application, the student is required to solve a problem in a new situation. As the student uses rules, laws, methods, or theories in a new situation (with a minimum of directions) transfer of learning occurs. Classroom examples include:

using writing skills (i.e. topic sentence,
   descriptive paragraph) to prepare a
   social studies report
using knowledge of the courtesies required in
   discussions by raising a hand in order
   to take a turn during the discussion

Analysis

In analysis the student breaks information
down into parts and identifies relationships between
the parts. Doing so, the student is better able to
understand the organization of information, draw
conclusions, and support them with evidence.
Classroom examples include:
   comparing and contrasting the personalities of
      Hamlet and Romeo
   classifying the elements of the play "Sorry,
      Wrong Number" into basic story
      categories

Synthesis

Here the student brings together several
pieces of information, ideas, or skills and arranges
them into a creative new whole. This is an act of
invention: combining elements into a structure that
was not there before. Classroom examples include:
   proposing an hypothesis and designing an
      experiment to test it
   devising a plan to solve the problem of
      landfills

Evaluation

In evaluating, the student makes a judgment
and gives reasons to support that particular position.
The criteria, either given to or determined by the
student, become the standard of appraisal and is
used to determine the validity of the judgment.
Classroom examples include:

choose the U.S. President you believe to be
most effective and state why
take a position on the capital punishment
issue; support it

Check Yourself Out!

Before we give you more classroom examples
of the taxonomy, practice thinking about Bloom's at
each of the six levels. Perhaps you'll experience the
increasing complexity of this hierarchy of cognitive
skills. Beginning with the lowest level:

Your knowledge. List the six levels of Bloom's
Taxonomy:
1.
2.
3.
4.
5.
6.

Your understanding. We'll give you a classroom
example; you tell us what level it is:

_____The student compares today's
religious unrest in Ireland with
the Crusades.

_____The student must decide whe-
ther religious wars should be
fought at all and tell why.

_____The student names the impor-
tant leaders of the Crusades.
The student defines, in his/her
own words, the terms Holy
Land, truce, pilgrimage.

_____The student suggests how life might be different if the Crusades were fought today.

_____The student writes a short story in which there is a dramatic new ending to the Crusades.

Your application. Explain several ways that your knowledge and understanding of Bloom's Taxonomy might improve your own teaching:

_____

_____

_____

_____

Your analysis. Here's a toughy--Compare and contrast Bloom's Taxonomy with Barrett's Taxonomy.

_____

_____

_____

Your synthesis. The levels of thinking as identified by Bloom do not always provide nice, discrete categories into which we can classify the level of thinking demanded of students. Design a new and better classification system of the cognitive domain.

_____

_____

_____

_____

Your evaluation. Should all teachers be required to know and understand Bloom's Taxonomy? Support your answer.

_____

_____

_____

Check your answers:

Knowledge. The six levels of Bloom's Taxonomy are knowledge, understanding, application, analysis, synthesis, evaluation.

Understanding. Your answers should be:
    analysis (clue word: compare)
    evaluation (decide/tell why)
    knowledge (names)
    understanding (defines in own words)
    application (principles of Crusades used
        today)
    synthesis (writes story with original ending)

Application. True application would really be to use Bloom's in your own instruction. It would affect your selection of objectives, your teaching behaviors and the kinds of behaviors you ask of students. Even the kinds of adjustments you make based on student responses would be influenced by your knowledge of Bloom's.

Analysis. Were you able to see similarities between Bloom's and Barrett's taxonomies? Or did you read the question and not even attempt it because you lacked the requisite knowledge? We purposely tried to include an area you would <u>not</u> be able to analyze so you could see that if a student does not have the knowledge and understanding of the content, it is futile to ask for analysis or any other higher cognitive level.

Synthesis. Did you find this a difficult, if not impossible task? Let's analyze the thinking that would be required to accomplish this task:

* you would need a good understanding of Bloom's (better than you could acquire from reading these few pages)
* perhaps you've tried using Bloom's to categorize the kinds of objectives you're teaching and to label the kinds of thinking you are getting from your students
* then, you probably did an analysis of the utility of Bloom's as a tool for classifying objectives and activities
* still in the analysis stage, you begin listing the strengths and weaknesses of Bloom's
* now, you are probably ready to develop some original ideas of your own--finally the synthesis level!

Have you gained an appreciation for the amount of time required for this level of thinking, as well as the increasing complexity of thought required? If you were able to accomplish this activity and you have a new taxonomy that you feel is better than Bloom's, we urge you to publish and share it with the rest of us!

Evaluation. You've made it to the last level of cognition according to Bloom! If this is true evaluation, there should be no right or wrong answer to the problem suggested. A few statements you might have made in support of your position:

NO! The objectives and curriculum are established already in our district; higher levels of thinking are provided; this information is most necessary for curriculum specialists.

NO! We use another taxonomy in our district which we feel is better because....

NO! Only teachers who are genuinely interested in learning the taxonomy will actually use it, so why require it at all? The questions in our textbooks are already labeled using the taxonomy.

YES! Teachers need to be aware there are other levels of thinking beyond recall of information. Bloom's provides a task analysis or a sequence for teaching and lesson planning. For example, knowledge and understanding must precede any higher level activity.

YES! It provides a tool to assist the teacher in individualizing. For example, within a lesson on multiplication, the teacher can ask a recall question of students needing practice at that level and give a word problem to students who already have the knowledge base.

YES! It aids the teacher in making adjustments in teaching. For example, if a student is not able to analyze, perhaps the teacher needs to go back and provide more instruction at the knowledge and understanding level OR the teacher may need to teach that student the thinking skill of how to analyze...more on this later.

Here's one last check of *your* understanding before we move on. Try explaining verbally what this graphic representation of Bloom's Taxonomy is all about (label each graphic; explain why you selected that label).

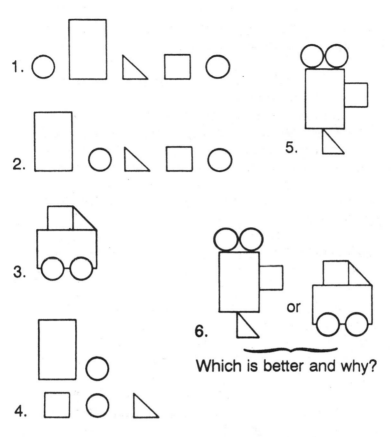

Your explanation may have sounded like this:

These graphics follow the order or levels of Bloom's:
#1 represents some isolated bits of information
(knowledge)
#2 simply rearranges the information; it still
resembles the original (comprehension)
#3 took the original information and used it in a
helpful way, a vehicle (application)
#4 the original information is categorized (analysis)
#5 something new and different has been created, a
projector (synthesis)
#6 requires a judgment—which is a better creation,
the vehicle or projector (evaluation)

Classroom Examples

Let's examine several classroom examples of teachers using Bloom's as a tool for sequencing lesson activities and extending students' thinking.

<u>Content: Nutrition and the food pyramid</u>
Knowledge: Name the levels of the food pyramid. Recall examples of food in each and the proportion of food required for a balanced meal.

Understanding: Given several examples of meals, pick the one best representing a well-balanced meal.

Application: Write a menu for you and your family for one week.

Analysis: Conduct "rate experiment"—one group fed milk, the other cola. Compare the growth patterns. Examine a menu from your favorite fast food restaurant and determine what could be ordered to provide balanced meals.

Synthesis: Identify an unusual situation (on a skiing trip, long boat trip, etc.) in which it would be difficult to get food. Plan how a well-balanced meal could be obtained.

Remember that overlapping we talked about? The following examples use knowledge and understanding; we'll combine activities that are difficult to group into one major category, called "higher levels."

<u>Content: World food problem; limitation of resources</u>
Knowledge: Watch a film and read the text to find evidence of the world food problem and possible causes.

Understanding: Outline the film and reading material.

Higher levels: Role play the consequences of applying one given solution to the problem (i.e., if a solution were to divide all food equally among nations of world, have students divide one piece of bread equally among themselves). Analyze the consequences of this solution and rank order potential solutions. Write a proposal selecting the best solution, supporting your decision.

You may be wondering why we "lumped" levels after understanding into "higher levels." The categories are not discrete. There is much overlap. In fact, some types of thinking represent a combination of skills that cut across Bloom's categories. The important thing to remember now is that it is critical to provide knowledge and understanding before extending students to higher levels. Too often the teacher is so eager to extend thinking that knowledge and understanding are not carefully monitored first.

Back to Where We Started

Do you remember where we started out in this chapter? Our goal was to help you determine the level of complexity of the objective.

We needed to spend time developing your knowledge and understanding of the levels of complexity (as identified by Bloom) before we could ask you to apply this information in developing clearly defined objectives. In Chapter 2 we worked on selecting the content of the objective near the correct level of difficulty. When you have identified the content and the level of complexity, you have clearly defined the *learning* in an objective.

CONTENT + THOUGHT PROCESS = LEARNING

Here are some examples of "learnings." The content is in boldface type; the thought process is in parentheses.

> Write a **resume** (application)*
> Know the **types of novels** (knowledge)
> Compare and contrast **inductive reasoning and deductive reasoning** (analysis)*
> Understand the concept **polygon** (understanding)

> *note that the thought process is implied, not stated

Our process in selecting an objective is not complete yet! The terms *know* and *understand* are open to many different interpretations. We need to include in our objective an observable behavior. A model for a clearly defined objective, then, might look like this:

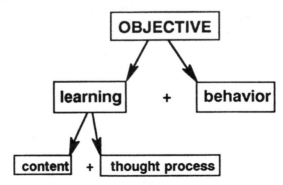

When the learning has been identified, you need to select the overt behavior that will show you that that learning has taken place. Just *any* overt behavior won't do! It must be *congruent,* match the thought process in the learning. If the thought process is at the knowledge level, matching overt behavior might be to write or say the information in the approximate form it was learned:

- **knowledge** of the Gettysburg Address: by **writing it down**

The kind of observable behavior you expect to see changes with the increasing complexity of the thought process. That is, if you change the thought process, you must also change the overt behavior:

- to **understand** the Gettysburg Address: by **explaining in own words** the meaning of the document

Next are some word indicating overt behaviors that (usually but not always!) match each level (or thought process). Remember that you may encounter a word like "compare" in objectives and one objective may require comprehension whereas another will require analysis.

Knowledge

Write
List, name
Label
Define
Be able to locate information

Understanding

Summarize
Give an explanation for
In your own words, describe
Draw a picture of
Predict
Defend
Select examples from non-examples

Application

Develop a plan for
Propose a solution to
Demonstrate
Use

Analysis

Break into parts, describe the patterns
Clarify
Identify the patterns, issues

Synthesis

Design
Create
Compose
Invent a new way

Evaluation

Conclude and support that conclusion
Select the best and tell why
Criticize
Make a choice and justify your decision

Students must have **knowledge** of terminology
before they can be expected to **understand** it.

B. Bloom

The following are more examples of performance objectives. Notice how the observable behavior *matches* the thought process:

Thought Process + Content	*Observable Behavior*
TLWD (the learner will demonstrate) *knowledge* of numerical value of pi	by *writing* it correctly to hundredths (3.14)
TLWD *understanding* of the concept louder	by correctly *selecting* which of 2 tones was louder
TLWD *understanding* of the card catalog	by *explaining* its use in locating specific information
TLW be able to *apply* the skills of research writing	by *writing* a research paper

Check Yourself Out!

You need some practice right now selecting overt student behaviors that match the thought process you are after. How about starting out easy—just match the following behaviors to the thought processes.

Thought process + Content	*Overt Behavior*
_____to know the rules of parliamentary procedure	a. by conducting a discussion in accordance with the rules of order
_____to understand the rules of parliamentary procedure	b. by naming in order the rules of order
_____to apply the rules of parliamentary procedure	c. by paraphrasing the rules

Check your answers: b, c, a.

Now try creating your own overt behaviors:

1. The learner will apply the skill of writing performance objectives by

2. The learner will demonstrate knowledge of the parts of an objective by

3. The learner will demonstrate understanding of a clearly defined objective by

Check your answers:
> 1. writing a performance objective for a lesson he/she will teach
> 2. listing those parts
> 3. discriminating from a list of objectives those that are well-written from those that are poorly-written

Caution: Danger Ahead!
Let's assume you can write a clearly defined objective and that you're convinced of the need to provide higher level experiences (objectives) for your students. Does that mean they will automatically respond at a higher level...even when the knowledge and understanding levels are in place? Unfortunately, the answer is NO! In addition to providing the knowledge necessary for a higher level objective, you may have to teach the thinking skill necessary to manipulate that knowledge at a higher level. "One does not become proficient at thinking without explicit instruction also in how to execute the very precise skills or operations of which it consists"

(Beyer, 1987). Now, this is not a text on thinking skills so we will not attempt to delineate the various skills and strategies necessary for students to think at a higher level (Beyer does an excellent job of this in his text). We do, however, want you to recognize when a thinking skill might be needed in order to teach a higher level objective. For example, consider this objective:

The learner will propose a solution to the world food problem (synthesis/evaluation).

To accomplish this objective, you may need to teach the skill of decision making to your students. This becomes a new objective: The learner will be able to apply the steps in decision making. You will task analyze this new objective (as we practiced in Chapter 2):

Can the learner:
define the problem
describe possible solutions
compare the alternative solutions
rank-order the solutions
select the "best" solution(s)

You may then have to teach to this objective. Have students practice it with easy subject matter, before having them apply the skill to the more difficult content (the world food problem).

Examples of thinking skills and strategies include:

distinguishing fact from opinion
comparing/contrasting
summarizing
detecting bias
inductive/deductive reasoning
problem solving
analyzing
determining credibility of source

Check Yourself Out!

Try to recognize the thinking skills inherent in the following objectives:

    1. The learner will write a comparison of democracy and communism.

    2. The learner will evaluate the claims of three television commercials.

    3. The learner will summarize the plot of Romeo and Juliet.

Did you say: (1) comparing (2) distinguishing fact/opinion; detecting bias (3) summarizing? Yes, this makes your job doubly difficult: finding objectives within objectives. You ask: What are the strategies or cognitive processes necessary to accomplish this higher level objective? Now your students will not only need to know/understand the concepts of democracy and communism, they will also have to have practice with the skill of writing a comparison.

Summary

    We face a great challenge: We must provide the body of information necessary to prepare our students to be culturally literate as well as provide the opportunity for students to use this information in a wide variety of circumstances. Bloom's Taxonomy is a classification system for objectives that helps us not only in writing our objective clearly but in providing the appropriate intellectual experiences for our students.

A man's mind, once stretched by a new idea, never regains its original dimensions.
Oliver Wendell Holmes

Chapter 4

Teach to the Objective

Can you:
• explain the concept "congruent teacher behaviors"
• identify congruent student activities
• relate task analysis to teaching to an objective

Chapters 2 and 3 helped us clearly define where we are going (the objective). Now we must figure out how we're going to get there! This chapter will consider

-the importance of first selecting the objective
-teacher behaviors facilitating learning
-student activities facilitating learning
-how a task analysis can help

Which Teacher Decision Is Made First?
As we described the process of selecting an objective at the correct level of difficulty and complexity, did you ask yourself the question: Why are we starting with the *objective?* Let's look at what happens when a teacher doesn't start the planning process with an objective. The lesson has just begun:

Teacher: Let's talk about color today. I have many favorite colors. Who can tell me their favorite colors? (Several students list their favorite colors.) I'll bet you didn't know that red has a tendency to make you salivate or that blue makes you sleepy.

Teacher: Does anyone know what makes color? (no answer)

Teacher: I want everyone to make a color wheel now. Take the square piece of paper you have and fold it into fourths. Watch how I can cut a good circle without having to draw any lines. All you do is hold the paper by the corner and cut a curved shape like this (models). (All students try; several require new paper because of mistakes.)

Teacher: Now divide the circle into six pie shapes like this (models). Color every other pie shape: red, then yellow, then blue. Hold yours up when you are ready. Great! Those are called primary colors. Now color in the secondary colors: orange, green, and purple. When you finish, try spinning your color wheel on the end of your pencil and notice what happens to the colors!

End of lesson! When this teacher was asked what was being taught in the lesson, the answer was, "Oh, something about colors." This phrase, *something about colors* , is subject to many interpretations. What do you think the students learned? Take your pick....

> how to follow directions
> how to cut a circle
> how to divide a circle into sixths
> what a color wheel is
> what the primary colors are
> what the secondary colors are
> how secondary colors are formed

The teacher is not sure what was learned because the lesson was planned around *activities,* not around a clearly defined objective. Every activity had something to do with color! The *objective* has not been defined and refined enough to allow us to teach to it. It's only a general description of *content.* Think about going on a trip. You have to know what your destination is before you can pack your suitcase. Just "going on a trip" doesn't tell you whether to pack a parka or a swimming suit. "Something about colors" doesn't tell us whether to pack our lesson with a box of crayons, to make a color wheel, or to show the film *The Red Balloon.*

If you could turn back the clock and re-teach the lesson, what would you do first?

If you thought, "I need a clearly defined objective, a clear statement of where I'm going in the lesson," then you're right! If we substitute, "The students will be able to name the primary and secondary colors," for "Something about colors," we can do a better job of selecting the appropriate activities. We'll do a better job of teaching to the objective. In fact, more appropriate activities would be added:

-the teacher writes the names of the primary and secondary colors on the board

-the teacher gives the students practice in remembering the colors: "Hold up the three crayons from your box that are primary colors. I'll name a color, whisper whether it is primary or secondary."

Some of the activities from the original lesson may stay the same. The big difference is that more teacher and learner *time* will be spent on the identified learning. There is a direct relationship between the amount of time a student spends on task and the achievement of that task (Brophy, 1992). Unfortunately only a few seconds were spent *mentioning* primary and secondary colors in the original lesson; practice *time* was in folding, cutting, and coloring (none of which will improve knowledge of primary and secondary colors!).

If you want to increase student achievement (and we're making the assumption that this is an important educational goal), you can do two things:

Specify what the student is to learn (clearly define your objective).

Find ways to keep the student involved with the specific learning (plan teacher and student behaviors that lead to the accomplishment of that objective).

Sound simple? Did you know that this is not happening in most classrooms? One study indicated that only 28% of the teachers questioned considered the objective first, prior to teaching (Clark & Yinger, 1979). Instead, the teachers thought first of the content ("something about colors") and then student activities (make a color wheel).

This kind of planning reminds us of the story about the accomplished marksman. He was traveling on a back country road one afternoon on his way to his next tournament. He glanced over to the nearby farm buildings and did a double-take at the side of an old dilapidated barn. Amazingly enough, the side of that barn was covered with targets. In the center of each target a perfect bull's-eye. "Someone nearby has certainly got a superior eye," he thought. Always eager to improve his own techniques, he decided to inquire at the closest farmhouse as to the identity of the expert marksman. Responding to his knock was an elderly gentleman who also claimed to be the person responsible for the perfect bull's-eyes. He gladly took the visitor out to the field, along with his shotgun. Wasting no time, he positioned himself, took careful aim, and squeezed the trigger. Whereupon, he walked over to the side of the barn, located a pellet hole, picked up a bucket of paint, and proceeded to draw his target around the hole!

The teacher in the color wheel lesson was shooting in a general direction and then drew a target after the fact. Haven't we all been there at one time or another?

Luckily for some of us, many districts have already written performance objectives plus rubrics (scales) to establish promotion standards. The objective plus rubric is of tremendous help to a teacher in both establishing what to teach as well as how to evaluate student performance on the objective. It's what we do with these objectives and rubrics that counts, though. A special drawer for filing them that's opened only to file a new set is not enough! We need our objectives uppermost in our mind in every lesson. Consider the farmer's words to Rabbit in Updike's *Rabbit, Run*: "The only way to get somewhere, you know, is to figure out where you're going before you go there." That's what performance objectives help us do! The rubric lets us know if the student is right on the target or close to it.

Selecting CONGRUENT Teacher Behaviors

Teaching to an objective means that all teacher actions will assist the learner in accomplishing the objective. Actions include: explanations, questions, directions, activities, assignments, and responses to learner efforts. To develop the concept of *congruency*, let's start with a familiar example: your objective is to clean the classroom for Open House. The room is a mess and in short order parents will begin arriving. Behaviors that are *congruent* or will assist in accomplishing the objective might be erasing the chalkboard, putting books away, or clearing the top of your desk. You probably would decide against correcting papers or cleaning out the bottom "junk" drawer of your desk. If you selected the last two activities, your room probably would not look the way you want when parents start arriving!

Teaching is not different. We have goals to accomplish. We have a time schedule, too. We have days filled with necessary but nonacademic activities: lining up, quieting down, collecting and distributing materials, etc. These activities drastically reduce the time available for learning. At least 20% of the classroom day is spent in these types of activities (Doyle, 1983). Then, another 23% of classroom time is allocated to music, art, physical education, etc. (Rosenshine, 1980). That leaves less than 57% of the day allocated to the communication arts, math, science or social studies. And remember, allocating time is not the same thing as actual time on task! While the teacher may plan to spend time on a lesson, the student may be off task *or* the teacher's activities may not be congruent with the task (*and that's the focus of this chapter*). It's easy to measure allocated time on task and easy to spot a student who is off task. It calls for more precision, however, to measure *congruency* of teacher activities to the task. We must know the objective first.

Let's look at examples of activities that will or will not lead to the accomplishment of an objective.

Objective (TLW=the learner will)	Congruent	Non-congruent
TLW make letter M	explain how to make strokes for an M	color a mountain
TLW describe French Rev.	show film depicting major events of F. R.	explain how to build a guillotine
TLW identify a hexagon	show examples of hexagons	model how to use a protractor

...the student learns whats/he does.

Anderson & Faust

Check yourself out!

Do you recognize "teaching to the objective?" In the following description of a lesson, you need to identify congruent and non-congruent behaviors.

The objective: TLW be able to read and determine the meaning of words with prefixes. The teacher has explained what a prefix is, given the students some examples of prefixes and their definitions, and now wants to check understanding. Put a check by any of the following activities/questions that do not match the objective.

1. Jason, what does the prefix *un* mean?
2. Will this prefix work with this root word: *un correct?*
3. Who knows what the prefix *in* means?
4. How many words can you make up with this list of prefixes and root words?
5. Everyone read this word (points to *untie*).
6. For seatwork, let's have a race and see who can think up the most words using this list of prefixes: *un, in, re.*

Hopefully, you checked 2, 4, and 6. The objective does not call for students to be able to create their own words with prefixes or even know the rule (if there is one) for which root can be combined with which prefix. The skill is for them to be able to read and know the meaning of these words when they encounter them in their reading. What happened in this lesson is that the students spent more than half of their instructional time on a learning they not only weren't taught but didn't need to learn. To make matters worse, they spent time practicing errors. Here are some of the words they put on their papers:
unconnect unknow recess unhonest incupboard

Clarity and Congruency in Teacher Behaviors

If congruency is defined in terms of assisting the learner in mastering the objective, then teacher *clarity* can either facilitate or hinder the learner. That is, when a teacher is presenting information (explaining), the clarity of that presentation will influence achievement (Brophy & Good, 1986). Let's take the lesson on prefixes described above and demonstrate how in even the congruent choices identified above, the teacher's presentation of them may detract from the learning.

1. *Vagueness*: Kids, you *might* run into prefixes *sometime* in your textbooks. They *usually* are little syllables found sometimes at the beginning of words. They *probably* will be on your test *sometime*.

2. *False starts, halting speech*: Sometimes in your read*...uh*, when you pick up a book you don't know....*I mean you encounter a diffi....*a long word that looks like it's made up of *smaller...er...a* ...recognizable syllables....

3. *Discontinuity* (interjecting irrelevant comments during the presentation): Three examples of prefixes are re, un, and in. *Oh, by the way, did you remember we go to an assembly today? Don't let me forget the time.* Now, let's define "re" first.

4. *'uh'*: Webster, *uh*, defines "re" as, *uh*, again or anew. *Uh*, the prefix, *uh*, "un", means not. It can be formed, *uh*, with,*uh*, nouns, or *uh*, adjectives....

Wow! Do you get the feeling that the more precise we get in analyzing teacher behaviors, the more self conscious we'll feel when we finally get up in front of class to teach! Just look at what we're going to analyze next: student workbooks and assignments. Yes, even they need to be *congruent!*

Selecting Congruent Student Practice Materials

"Students achieve more in classes where they spend most of their time being taught or supervised by their teachers rather than working on their own...."(Brophy & Good, 1986). If this is the case, is that an accurate description of what's happening in classrooms? Unfortunately not: kids in grades one to seven spend between 50-75% of their day working alone, on independent seatwork (Rosenshine & Stevens, 1986). What's even more frustrating is the quality of the seatwork activities. While students need active practice in the learning...only congruent active practice promotes learning. In fact, requiring trivial practice can actually interfere with the learning (Brophy & Alleman, 1991).

The following are examples of such poor activities:

Objective: TLW recognize the fractional area 1/2.

Using your pencil, divide these shapes to show 1/2.

What's the problem with this activity? Recognizing the fractional area 1/2 is not the same skill as dividing a geometric shape into fractional parts. One student's paper looked like this:

Does this student really understand fractions? Or, was he given something so difficult, requiring skills he did not have, that he was unable to demonstrate his understanding of the simpler concept, one half.

Objective: TLW be able to add "ing" to words ending in "e" (i.e. like to liking).

Practice the new rule: drop "e" and add "ing"
   1. Min is_____her new bike.
   2. Edward is _____a chocolate cake.
   3. What will Lou _____in the stove?

make	making
bake	baking
ride	riding

There are two things wrong with this activity. The teacher doesn't know if the child can remember the rule because the word is already written as a model to copy! In addition, kids are being tested on their ability to discriminate between when to use a root word and when to use it with a suffix. Many student papers were filled in with: What will Lou *baking* in the stove? Can you figure out why?

Objective: TLW show understanding of vocabulary words by selecting the correct word for a given sentence.

---

1. The wealthy woman_____ the stairs.
         destiny   descended   desolation

2. Mercury was the_____of the gods.
      shrewdest   shrouded   shrugged

What's the problem? You don't even have to know the meanings of these words to get a perfect paper. Kids can read the sentence and fill in the word that "sounds" right. For the past tense, there's only one *ed* option; for the superlative form, there's only one *est*.

Now, we are going to tread on "motherhood and apple pie." That is, there are two categories of activities that are popular at all grade levels—and perhaps even more inappropriate than the ones described so far. But...they're revered by many. Teachers will say "Our kids love to do these!" Newton Minow (National Association of Broadcasters Meeting, 1961) would have an apt response to this: "If parents, teachers, and ministers conducted their responsibility by following the ratings, children would have a steady diet of ice cream, school holidays, and no Sunday School." What are the culprits? The *word search* and the *scrambled letter* worksheets.

Objective: TLW name musical instruments. (The following is only a portion of this word search.)

```
G O N G L O C
U B A L U R Y
A O A O T E M
T E O C E B B
```

What's the problem? This is only a word recognition task. The student is not asked to recall anything. The directions on this worksheet tell students that the words are upside down, horizontal, backwards, diagonal or vertical. Students with learning disabilities should not be asked to read upside down or backwards. In fact, when do we ever read this way? We can't even use the excuse that a word search helps develop fluency in reading...it does exactly the opposite. Our written language has a very strong visual clue to help us with fluency: space between words. What does a word search do? It deprives us of this valuable visual marker.

Tryreadingthissentencewiththesameeaseandfluencyyou'vebeenusing.

This is not a condemnation of all word searches. Why might the following search be more appropriate:

Objective: TLWBAT visually identify vowels.

```
b  m  t  u  a  t
e  x  i  w  i  l
p  q  l  x  o  a
```

Did you say: Students are working with isolated letters, not words, and the letters are evenly spaced; students can scan from left to right; they are not asked to read upside down or backwards?

    Scrambled letters: No grade level is immune from this type of activity. They're even found in foreign language classes!

Objective: TLW know vocabulary words.

Unscramble these words to find your new vocabulary words.
sacerela   rasnecso   lavel   catador

Don't these words look foreign enough already? Why do we make the task of learning foreign vocabulary even more difficult for students by having them, through a trial and error process, rearrange the letters to make another foreign word? About the only use for scrambled words would be to improve your skill in the game of Scrabble!

    You are still teaching to the objective when students are on independent practice. If your objective requires comprehension level or above thinking, make sure your practice activity does, too. Unfortunately, most commercially published activities ask for very low level thinking: color in, draw a circle around, underline, cut and paste.

Beware of activities that have students spending the majority of their time on unrelated activities, just to produce a related answer. That is, if students need to discriminate a plant cell from an animal cell, it's more efficient to show them two cells and ask them to label them. We found one workbook where students were asked to cut out puzzle pieces, glue them together, then decide if it was a plant or animal cell. Can we justify 95% of the time on trivia and 5% on the learning?

Elementary teachers, be particularly wary of materials prepared for young children. While teaching reading, writing, and arithmetic are still a major focus for these early grades, commercial materials have our students coloring or cutting and pasting the majority of the time. If one learns to read by *reading* or one learns to write by *writing*, doesn't it make more sense to get our students reading and writing?

When selecting practice activities, ask yourself the following questions:

1. What is my learning or objective?
2. What is the cognitive demand of this activity?
3. Does my objective match the cognitive demand of the task?
4. What percent of the time will students be engaged in trivial activities, not in pursuit of the intended learning?

Active responses which are irrelevant to the purpose of the lesson can interfere with learning.

Anderson & Faust

Easier said than done!

Just so you are not feeling too uncomfortable about now...wondering if it's really possible to teach to an objective and keep everything congruent, we'll share this thought with you:

While we know that the shortest distance between two points is a straight line (teaching to an objective)

TEACHING ⸻▶ OBJECTIVE

there always seems to be a curve in the road!

TEACHING 〜〜 OBJECTIVE

The principal comes on the PA system to make an announcement. The class clown decides to perform...in the middle of your lesson. A student comes in with an important message. Or, out of the blue, a student asks you if you watched the football game last night!

How do you deal with this? You choose: Make a *conscious* decision to abandon ship and discuss the new "objective" or decide to get back on target. Kids are masters at recognizing teachers not conscious of the concept of congruency. They actually plot how to get the teacher onto another subject. They'll pick a word search over having to write a descriptive paragraph. It's easier!

As you struggle in your efforts to teach to your objective, you'll find it's not just the kids who take you off task. As we discussed earlier, commercially published materials are filled with "busy work." No, you don't have to write your own materials. Even if you wanted to, where would you find the time? Keep this in mind: We want *material-proof* teachers because there are no *teacher-proof* materials. Hemingway said it best when asked what the essential ingredient of a good writer was: "In order to be a great writer a person must have a built-in, shockproof crap detector." Let's apply that to teaching: "In order to be a great teacher you must have a built-in, shockproof crap detector."

Task Analysis: The Key to Congruency

In Chapter 2 the idea of using a task analysis to find an objective near the correct level of difficulty was introduced. Task analysis can also be used to guide you in the selection of matching teacher/student behaviors. In Chapter 2 the focus was on task-analyzing long-range objectives; the same process applies to daily instructional objectives. Below is an example of a long range objective followed by an analysis of one of the component steps. The second task analysis is for a lesson plan that can be taught in one or two lessons, while the first is for a longer unit.

Long Range Objective:
TLWD understanding of parts of a book.

1. locates title, author, publisher, copyright date
2. explains use/organization of table of contents
3. explains use/organization of glossary
4. explains use/organization of index
5. explains use/organization of bibliography
6. can discriminate which part of book to use to locate specific information

Daily Instructional Objective:
TLWBAT use an index.
1. can locate index in a book
2. understands attributes of index
   arranged in alphabetical order
   gives page numbers
   identifies topics & subtopics
   abbreviations used
   may give many page listings
   may refer you to another topic
   may identify illustrations
3. given a topic, can use an index to find that
   information
4. given a question, can identify topic, then
   use index to find information

A set of blueprints is to the builder as a task analysis is to the teacher. That is, the task analysis of an instructional objective guides the teacher in selecting *matching* materials, activities, examples, or questions. If the step is "can locate an index in a book," it's easy to see that a *matching* student activity would be to have them find the index in a textbook, not to give them a word search in which to find the word "index"! The task analysis encourages a teacher to plan a lesson as a series of small incremental steps. It signals to the teacher when to stop and check student understanding of a step. On the next page is an example of a lesson plan model that is "guided" by the task analysis. For each step in the task analysis, the teacher plans congruent actions (input, model, etc.) as well as congruent activities for the students.

The lesson will flow from left to right, with teacher and student involvement for each substep. We call it the *three-prong model* for lesson planning.

TLWBAT use an index.		
Task Analysis	**Teacher Behavior**	**Student Processing**
1. knows location of index ➡	1. explain location; show examples➡	1. locate index in own book
2. knows attributes of an index ➡	2. list attributes; explains each; show each w/model on overhead ➡	2. points to each attribute in own index

How Far Back Do You Go?

At what point in student development does a long-term objective become a daily-instructional objective? This is a tough question to answer. Consider the objective: TLWBAT write a research paper. At the high school level, the steps of defining the topic or locating information may be sufficient detail for students to accomplish with minimal difficulty and very little teacher instruction. A major decision for the teacher will be the amount of time to allot to completion of the assignment. However, an elementary teacher would probably view each of these steps as a long range objective. For example, the step of locating information requires students to know how to use various resources (i.e., general reference books, card catalogue, vertical file). To be able to use general reference books means the ability to use a dictionary, thesaurus, almanac, etc. Each of these can be further task analyzed into subskills—all the way down to locating entry words in a dictionary. The process could go on indefinitely. Anderson and Faust (1973) address the issue of just how detailed a task analysis should be: "When a student can perform the component skill upon simply being asked to do it, then the skill has been analyzed in sufficient detail."

Flexible Subgroups

Another approach to the seemingly infinite process of task analysis is to establish developmental milestones against which to measure individual student progress. Given the diversity that exists in classrooms today it is virtually impossible to have all students on the same step of the task analysis at the same time. For example, developmental indicators for writing are established (via task analysis). In the area of mechanics, these might begin with subskills:

The Beginning Writer

TL consistently begins sentences with capital letters

TL uses invented phonetic spellings

TL uses short, simple sentences

The Intermediate Writer

TL consistently begins sentences with capitals

TL usually spells words correctly—misspelled words being phonetically correct

TL uses both simple and compound sentences

This task analysis can be used to diagnose individual students on what subskill they need next. The task analysis can be used to identify flexible groupings of students who are in need of a particular step.

Teaching to an objective does not imply direct instruction to the whole class. It includes teaching flexible small groupings of students as well as planning opportunities for students to learn *on their own*—indirect instruction. The key is that the instructional opportunity be congruent with the objective.

Summary

Teaching to an objective helps us increase time on task. It's knowing where you are going and picking the most efficient way to get there. By including only *congruent* teacher and student actions in a lesson we have not only made better use of our time in the classroom, we've made learning easier for our students. In particular, student activities need to be examined to see if they match the intended objective.

A task analysis guides the selection of congruent teacher and student behaviors. The three-prong lesson format guides us in our lesson planning.

The great thing in this world is not so much where we are, but in what direction we are moving.
Oliver Wendell Holmes

TLWBAT locate any fiction book on the shelf.

Task Analysis	Teacher Behavior	Student Processing
1. know difference between fiction/non-fiction	1. explain using words true/not-true; give ex. of Star Wars, A.Lincoln, Goldilocks	1. all signal 1 or 2 to discriminate fiction/non-f.
2. know call number	2. show location/many books; draw model; give ex. of kid's last names	2. point to call # on own book; write call # with own name
3. know books on shelf in alph. order by call #	3. relate to order in dictionary; write ex. on board	3. in coop. team, put books in order on table
4. can find book on shelf	4. point out order of shelves in library	4. given title & author, locate book

Given 2 magazine articles, TLWBAT write a comparison.

Task Analysis	Teacher Behavior	Student Processing
1. introduce subject/ topic	1. explain with 2 familiar articles; put introduc. on overhead	1. individually read 2 short articles; write intro.
2. discuss ways they are identical or similar	2. list similarities of same 2 articles on OH; show a completed paragraph	2. make a list of similarities; write a paragraph
3. discuss ways they are different or contra-dict	3. list differences; show a completed paragraph	3. make a list of differences; write paragraph
4. general summary	4. list what's included in summary; show model	4. write general summary

Given a money amount orally, TLWBAT write the amount using standard decimal notation for dollars and cents.

Task Analysis	Teacher Behavior	Student Processing
1. know that money amts. have $ to left of #s	1. explain; show on board	1. write in $, give #s only (3.75)
2. use $ for money only	2. give ex. of difference between general #s and #s as money	2. given ex., sig-nal when to use $ (I have 2 cars. It costs 2 dollars.)
3. after $, write numeral for # of dollars	3. explain/model	3. given only $ amounts, write ($3)
4. use a decimal point to separate $ & cents	4. explain; many ex.; point to a side, kids name which	4. given $ and cents, write ($4.75)
5. use "00" if no cents	5. explain; model on chalkboard	5. given $ amts., write ($3.00)
6. use a "0" preceding numeral for cents 1-9	6.explain; model on chalkboard	6. given amounts, write ($3.08)

Chapter 5

Monitor and Adjust

Can you:
• list & describe monitoring strategies
• explain the steps in monitoring & adjusting
• explain "feedback and correctives"
• give examples of when to monitor

Have you heard the ad that begins something like "40 million people can't be wrong"? We can't make quite that claim for this chapter but we can quote scholars in education and their syntheses of the research on good teaching to defend the importance of monitoring and adjusting.

Let's review where we are. We have selected our objective (level of difficulty and level of complexity) and we are teaching to that objective. Now, listen to the researchers:

Porter & Brophy (1988): "Effective teachers continuously monitor their students' understanding of presentations and responses to assignments. They routinely provide timely and detailed feedback...."

Rosenshine (1986): "Effective teachers also stop to check for understanding by posing questions...."

Evertson et al. (1980): The most effective junior high math teachers asked an average of 24 questions during a 50-minute period; the least effective teachers asked an average of 8.6 questions.

Mager (1968) put it another way: "If telling were the same as teaching, we'd all be so smart we could hardly stand it." Without monitoring and adjusting, we'd be in the "telling" mode.

Slavin (1988) appeals to our common sense: "Imagine an archer who shoots arrows at a target but never finds out how close to the bull's-eye the arrows fall. The archer wouldn't be very accurate to begin with, and would certainly never improve in accuracy."

Of the variables that influence learning, frequent assessment and feedback are ranked among the most important (Wang et al., 1994). Monitoring is the process of assessing and evaluating learning as it is taking place. We can't afford to wait until a project is turned in or the unit exam is given to measure the learning. In many cases it's too late to make adjustments.

Making the assumption that we value the need to monitor our students, let's refine the skill. The first issue is:

Whom Should We Monitor?

Wouldn't you like to teach so that *all* of your students learn the material? You wouldn't purposely exclude students from the opportunity to learn. Yet, unknowingly, this may be the case in some classrooms. When teachers ask questions to monitor student understanding, high achievers are most likely to be called upon (Good, 1970). Low achievers are less frequently encouraged to participate in class discussion or interact with the teacher. If most of our questions are directed to the top third (academically) of our class, then whose understanding are we checking? What about the other two-thirds of the class?

How Many Students Should We Monitor?

Did you ever take a class in experimental psychology? Remember how experimental data were reported? You would first read about the sample size or how many subjects participated in the experiment. This was generally reported as the "n" or number involved (i.e., n=345; n= 27). What would you think of a study with an n=1? Not a very large sample! You probably wouldn't put much value in the data.

When we monitor student learning, we are "taking a sample" from the whole population (our class). Do you know what our most common sample size is? Did you say "n=1"? And to think that we make decisions whether to go on with our lesson or go back and reteach based on this limited information! Worse yet, combine this with the research cited above (questions directed to the top third of our class). Could we improve our monitoring strategies?

Monitoring Strategies

If we're to monitor all levels of students (high, middle, and low) and get a larger sample size as a measure of the learning, we need to look at the strategies we're using. The old standby (ask a question and call on the first hand up) just won't do for monitoring or measuring the amount of learning. It's a fine strategy if the goal is to encourage class discussion or stimulate curiosity; but for the purposes of this chapter, it is not sufficient! Let's expand our repertoire of strategies to check understanding and measure student learning. Examples include:

1. choral responding (verbal response)
2. signal the answer (using thumbs up, down, & sideways; point; show # with fingers)
3. write answer down (on scratch paper; think pad)

4. discuss answer (with a team; partner or "study buddy")

Here's what these strategies would sound like.

Choral responding refers to any verbal, whole or small group response:
"All of you whisper the answer."
"Row 3, tell me how many."

Signals include:
"Using your magic chalkboard (chest), show me how many seasons there are."
"Thumbs up if it's figurative; down if literal; sideways if you're not sure."
"Make a fist for a period or put your pointer finger up for an exclamation mark. Now, show me how you'd punctuate these sentences."
"Using your pencil, put it upright on your desk if the answer is true; keep it down if false." (This works well with secondary students.)

Writing includes:
"On a piece of scratch paper, write an example of a topic sentence for a paragraph on tropical plants."
"On your think pad, solve this equation."

Discuss includes:
"Turn to your study partner and describe the Renaissance."
"In your team, analyze the issues involved and decide who had the greatest advantages in the Civil War."
"Turn to the person next to you and each give two examples of mammals."

These strategies or variations of them have both advantages as well as disadvantages. And, like everything else in teaching, their use is contextual. That is, they'll be appropriate in one situation but not in another.

Cognitive Level and "Think Time"

Two other variables need to be considered that will help us in our choice of monitoring strategies: cognitive level of the question and "think time" needed to answer. Yes, it's back to Bloom's Taxonomy! When we monitor student learning, the question is: What level of learning are we measuring? If you want to know whether students can remember certain facts, you're measuring the knowledge level. If you are "checking for understanding" you are measuring the comprehension level. And so on....up the taxonomy. If you want to monitor your students' analyses of the Civil War, you probably wouldn't select the thumbs up strategy! Yet, if you need to be sure they remember the major issues involved, thumbs up might be useful.

"Class, I'll name an issue. If it was a major issue in the Civil War, thumbs up. If not, down. If you're not sure, sideways. First, slavery?"

The time needed for students to think of the answer, to give you an accurate measure of their learning, will also vary with the level of the question. First, though, we'll examine the research on *think time.*

Typically, when teachers ask questions, they leave less than one second before calling on a student for an answer (Rowe, 1987). Wow! That's barely time for the student to repeat the question to himself, let alone construct an answer. The answer the teacher is likely to get is probably not an accurate measure of that student's learning. Rowe found that if teachers can lengthen the think time (she calls it "Wait-Time I") to an average of more than three seconds that:

- •the length of the student response will increase ("That student knew more than I thought....")
- •the number of unsolicited but appropriate responses increases (A bigger sample....)
- •failures to respond decrease ("Ah, she knew after all....")
- •confidence in response increases ("It's not just a lucky guess....")
- •speculative and inferential thinking increases (higher level thinking....)
- •frequency of student questions increases ("Their questions help me make adjustments....")
- •more answers are given by "slow" students (a more representative sample; "Perhaps I've misjudged that student!")

If the quality of our monitoring improves with the addition of but a few seconds of silence, isn't it worth trying?

The *length* of the wait time is going to depend upon the level of thinking you want to monitor or measure. A simple recognition question (Was slavery an issue....) may need only 3 seconds, but when you want to test analytical thinking, students will need minutes. Again, this will also influence your choice of monitoring strategy. Discussing an answer in a small group or writing on a scratch paper will allow for that valuable think time and provide a more accurate measure of that type of thinking.

Check Yourself Out!

If you're going to develop a larger repertoire of monitoring strategies, you'll first need to analyze where and when they'll be most appropriate. Fill in the grid, comparing the 4 strategies on the issues of sample size, appropriate cognitive levels, as well as general advantages and disadvantages of the strategy.

	choral	signal	write	discuss
sample size				
cognitive levels				
advantages +				
disadvantages -				

Did your answers include:

Choral responding can sample the entire class. The problem is that it's easy to "fake" an answer and the teacher can't be sure who knows and who doesn't. At best, it gives an approximate measure of the learning: a loud, confident answer versus a few voices with question-like tones! It also works best with low level questions that have only a one or two word answer. It's one of the most efficient strategies in terms of time, and, at the same time, can be very difficult to implement well. You need a cue (i.e., look at me when you're ready with an answer) to build in the necessary think time before getting the choral answers. Even with a cue, some students just blurt out the answers, allowing others to just "echo."

Signals can get a whole class sample. If the teacher requires students to keep the signal against the chest, it's more difficult to copy or to hide, as you can in choral responses. Signals work best with true-false questions, multiple choice questions, or questions where a symbol or letter can be formed with the hand (i.e., long or short vowel sound; number of syllables; question mark or period). It's more difficult to measure higher level thinking with a signal answer. Older students may challenge the technique ("If you agree, give me one finger....") If you do use it with secondary students, let them know they have the option of letting you measure their understanding this way or by responding in writing, as a homework assignment! Given that choice, do you want to predict what they'll choose?   Signals should also be used sparingly; they can get rather boring! Yet, they are efficient in terms of use of time and easy to monitor (just do a visual scan of the class). Again, the teacher has to cue the students when to signal, to allow for sufficient think time.

Writing the answer out allows for a whole class sample. It lends itself to all cognitive levels of questions. But it definitely takes more time to walk up and down aisles to monitor the answers. You aren't likely to look at every answer; therefore, sample size is reduced. It's easy to individualize for think time, though, because the student isn't likely to begin writing without thinking first!

Discussing or verbally sharing an answer with a peer or team again allows for a sample size of at least half the class.   The problem is getting around to enough students to hear the answers! This will reduce your sample size somewhat. Timewise, it's more efficient than writing. You can answer higher level questions in less time verbally than it takes to write them out. It does allow for all levels of questions. Think time is easier to control when compared to choral responding or signaling; it's built into the strategy.

"Think-Pair-Share." No, this is not a new strategy. It is a combination of strategies that includes think time, sharing your thoughts with a partner, and sharing your thoughts with the whole class. When students learn this three-step procedure, the teacher merely has to signal which step (i.e., point to head for think; cross fingers when it's time to pair up; raise hand when it's time to share with whole class). While partners are sharing with each other, the teacher can be monitoring the variety of responses (McTighe & Lyman, 1988).

Steps in Monitoring and Adjusting
Now that we've looked at all the variables influencing the quality of our monitoring and examined monitoring strategies, let's look at the process itself. What steps do you go through?

1. **Elicit (get) congruent overt behavior from the learner.**
2. **Check the behavior.**
3. **Interpret the behavior.**
4. **Act on the interpretation.**

Elicit congruent overt behavior. In order to check the learning, we have to see the behavior. Many times we ask the question, "Do you understand?" or, "Is that clear?" Students might shake heads, raise hands or even give us blank looks. Questions like these do not give us proof of the learning. In fact, if you want to get picky about it (and we do!), the only thing you know for sure by asking those questions is that students know how to shake heads, raise hands, or give blank looks!

Now's the time to use one of the four strategies described earlier. Remember, though, even with one of those strategies, the behavior must be *congruent* with the learning you're measuring. If you're teaching a lesson on proper nouns and you want to see if the students can discriminate them from common nouns, you might say:

"I'll give you three words. Show me with the appropriate number of fingers which of the three is a proper noun. STUDENT FOOTBALL CHICAGO".

Here's another example of getting overt behavior for the above example. Is it congruent?

"I'm going to give you a scrambled word. Write it down on your thinkpad; unscramble it. Is it a proper noun?"

Did you emphatically say "NO"? We hope so. While you used a good strategy (writing), the overt behavior is not congruent with learning to discriminate proper nouns. It's merely a trial and error exercise of rearranging letters to make a word.

Check the behavior. It's so easy to ask students to discuss an answer or write something and then yourself forget to look at or listen to the responses. Instead, you use the time to put something on the chalkboard or talk to a single student. Checking the behavior means to look at or listen to as many answers as possible (remember sample size?) because your next responsibility is to....

Interpret the behavior. Do the answers students are giving match the intended learning? Rosenshine (1986) classifies student responses as
- correct, quick, and firm
- correct, but hesitant
- incorrect, but a "careless" error
- incorrect, suggesting lack of knowledge of facts or a process

Whether you've called upon a single student or you are looking at a whole class response, these categories can be helpful in deciding how you'll act on the interpretation. With whole group responses, the interpretation is more difficult because rarely do you get 100% agreement on answers. What do you do if 50% have a correct answer and the other 50% are not correct?

Act on the interpretation. What do you do now? Adjust the level of difficulty? Move on? Reteach? Abandon ship? This is by far the most difficult decision in the monitoring and adjusting process. Unfortunately, one study found that "teachers rarely changed their strategy from what they had planned, even when instruction was going poorly" (Clark & Yinger, 1979). Damn the torpedoes, full speed ahead? Hopefully not.

Rosenshine suggests the following teacher responses to his four types of student answers:

Correct, quick, and firm: Provide feedback "Yes, the answer is...." Continue on with the lesson, either by asking another question or teaching the next step in your task analysis. The goal is to maintain momentum and pacing.

Correct, but hesitant: Now we not only give feedback as to the accuracy of the answer "Yes, that's right," but we add information related to how the answer was formulated. "Yes, it is figurative because it is so exaggerated; it couldn't possibly be true."

Incorrect, but careless: Remember momentum and pacing. Give the correct answer and continue on with the lesson. "No, that is a proper noun."

Incorrect (lack of knowledge or understanding of process): You have two choices here: prompting or reteaching. Try a prompt if it is brief. Don't lose momentum and pacing by losing the students who knew the answer. Reteach, however, if you have a high error rate.

One of the easiest times to reteach is when the students who have mastered the learning move on to independent practice. Pull aside the students who need additional help. If you use cooperative team learning, here is an opportunity to have those students in the team who have mastered the learning tutor those who haven't. There is a positive relationship between giving help in a team (tutoring) and achievement, so you are not "holding back" the student who had the correct answer (Webb, 1982).

Rosenshine emphasizes that whether you choose to reteach or provide prompts/hints, the critical thing is that *errors should not go undetected*.

When Should We Monitor?

Frequently! Perhaps our best guide is the task analysis of the lesson. When you have taught one step, which is a prerequisite to the next step, *monitor*. Why move on to the next sub-learning, if the previous one has not been mastered? We all know how difficult it is to correct a problem when it has been practiced incorrectly for a period of time. In mastery learning, students take formative quizzes every week or two. Correctives are provided (if necessary) and they must master an alternative form of the same quiz before moving on to the next objective.

We'd suggest monitoring on an even more frequent schedule. If you have three major points to get across in your 50 minute lecture today, measure the learning after each point! If you are teaching three or four sequential steps to a math process during a 30-minute lesson, you might consider monitoring after each step! Again, the decision is contextual. Two teachers with the same task analysis may monitor at different times. One may stop after the first step to measure student learning because the learners in that class are very heterogeneous and find the topic difficult. The second teacher, who has a class of "gifted" learners, teaches three steps before monitoring. We'll give you more clues as to when to monitor in the chapter on retention.

Monitoring Student-Directed Activities

Monitoring during direct instruction is actually easier than during student-directed activities. That is, when students are in literature clubs, learning centers, working on projects, or involved in writers' workshop, you could potentially have each student on a different objective! How do you consistently (not eventually) monitor them?

When students are at learning centers (which, by the way, should have a clearly defined objective with congruent practice activities), the teacher practices "clipboard cruising". With a clipboard to record your observations, become a roving monitor. You can provide feedback—correctives as you monitor.

When students are working independently in readers' or writers' workshop, establish a schedule whereby each student is conferenced once a week. Post the schedule. You'll probably be able to see five or six students a day for about 5 minutes per conference.

If students are working on a "menu" of activities or objectives that are self-paced, have a place in the room (i.e., a chart or whiteboard) for them to sign up for a conference with you when one of their objectives is accomplished. Be ever vigilant, however, for the student who doesn't sign up regularly for a conference! We know of one teacher who spends one day a week monitoring those students who haven't voluntarily signed up!

Summary

Monitoring and adjusting is analogous to measuring the learning and doing something with the results of that measurement. While all teachers monitor, the questions are: *who* is monitored in the class, how many are monitored, and *how* are students monitored. Our goal in this chapter was to refine our monitoring strategies to include the greatest number of students, giving them all time to think of an answer, and then acting appropriately on their answers. Errors should not go undetected! Feedback and correctives are provided with each response.

Mistakes are a fact of life.
It is the response to error that counts.
Nikki Giovanni

Principles of Learning

In Chapters 6-9 we will take a look at principles of learning. These general propositions about learning assist in applying psychology to education.

RETENTION...what principles will affect remembering?

MOTIVATION...what principles affect the focus of students?

ACTIVE PARTICIPATION...what can we do to affect the rate and amount of learning?

MENTAL SET...how can the combination of retention, motivation, and active participation get students ready to learn?

Using principles of learning effectively makes the teacher more than a provider of information. The teacher-learner relationship becomes dynamic. Proactively, the teacher makes decisions about building in meaning...or modeling...or level of concern to influence the learning of students. Reactively, the teacher responds to learner efforts by providing knowledge of results...or praise...or increases the level of difficulty to, again, influence the learning of students.

We'll provide lots of practical suggestions for the use of principles of learning. Their ultimate use, though, is up to you. Decisions must be made as to when, where, and with whom they are appropriate.

The Fall, 1993 issue of *Review of Educational Research* considered the question: Can research inform practice? After Wang et al. presented a knowledge base for school learning (a synthesis of factors that influence student learning), other researchers cautioned about moving directly from the general principle to the application. The principle only suggests applications—*teachers* need to make adjustments to meet the special demands of their unique situation. For example, Ibuprofen is a known pain reliever. Before this knowledge can be put to use, the medical characteristics of the patient as well as the dosage must be considered. Giving Ibuprofen to a kidney patient can be harmful. Similar adjustments have to be made before general principles of learning can become guides to assist student learning.

Chapter 6

Retention

Can you:
- **explain how brain structure influences learning**
- **explain "information processing" as it relates to retention**
- **give examples of**
  modeling—multiple modalities
  meaning
  processing
  ***effective* practice**

Why have a new computer if you don't know how to use it? Imagine having the most sophisticated computer available and yet being able to do only word processing on it! The ultimate capacities of that machine are left untapped. Teachers are working with a machine far more sophisticated than any computer: the human mind. Unless we understand how it works, we are unlikely to even begin to tap its potential.

One example of this tremendous potential is the suggestion that our long-term memory is capable of storing as much information as found in all the libraries of the world! Or, there is the assertion that we probably use less than one percent of our brain's capacity. This chapter will focus primarily upon the brain's capacity for remembering information. In particular, four variables under teacher control that can improve memory: modeling/multiple modalities, meaning, processing and practice. Instead of simply presenting the variables with associated strategies, we will link each variable to brain structure and organization.

Original Learning +	Practice	= Retention
1. modeling, multiple modalities 2. meaning 3. processing	1. amount 2. when 3. how 4. feedback	

Geography of the Brain

Although our three-pound machine is composed of tens of billions of cells, it is remarkably well organized. Looking at the machine from the bottom up, from the oldest part of the brain to the newest, we see: (1) the reptilian complex (taking care of automatic functions of the body like blood pressure & temperature); (2) the limbic system (taking charge of emotions and perhaps short-term memory); (3) then the upper brain, the cerebral cortex. It's the cerebral cortex that interests us most as educators because it is vital to learning and memory.

The cortex, over 80-85% of our brain mass, allows us to store new information as well as contemplate the future. Just as the brain has specialized functions from the bottom up, so too does the cortex specialize from the front to the back. The frontal lobes participate in planning for the future. The parietal lobes, on the top of the cortex, process motor activities and sensations (i.e., touch, pain). The temporal lobes, above both ears, appear to help file information into long-term memory as well as process auditory information. The occipital lobes, at the back of the head, are responsible for visual processing.

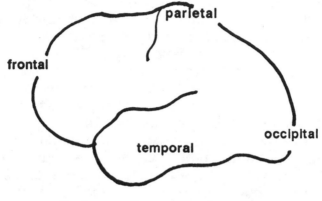

Lobes of cerebral cortex

Adding more specialization to an already specialized cerebral cortex, the cortex is divided into cerebral hemispheres. In general, the left hemisphere is responsible for language, speech, analytical and sequential information while the right hemisphere appears to process visual-spatial information and deal with information simultaneously.

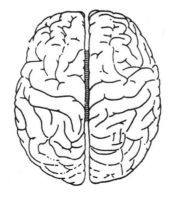

language		visual
speech		spatial
analytic		simultaneous
sequential		pattern
LEFT		**RIGHT**

HEMISPHERES

Why bother with this description of the brain? With an appreciation of the complexity of this machine comes an awareness of the many ways information can be processed and stored. Are we tapping the potential of the brain in our lessons? Goodlad (1984) found that at the high school 70% of instructional time in classrooms involved teacher "talk." Of the remaining time, only 1.7% involved demonstrations, .2% simulation and role playing and 2.9% the use of audio-visual equipment. Sylwester (1995) argues that we need to provide a classroom environment that activates the whole brain.

The PET scanner, a sophisticated machine that identifies areas of the brain activated during any activity, demonstrates the cumulative nature of tasks. It's like a light bulb, lighting up that section of the brain being used. For example, reading a word (a noun) silently lights up but a small area of the cortex. Saying the word lights up more. Generating a verb to go with the noun lights up even more! If you were to use a scanner to measure the areas of learners' brains activated during your teaching, what would you find? Are you providing multiple opportunities for learning?

Modeling—Multiple Modalities

This first principle of retention theory refers to multi-sensory input such as demonstrations, pictures, visual-spatial input. We are assuming that verbal activities are in place (70% of the time according to Goodlad): reading from a textbook, listening to a lecture, answering questions verbally or in writing. Can you balance this instruction with nonverbal kinds of knowledge, tactual-kinesthetic experiences and visualization activities. Field trips give the opportunity for this multi-sensory approach.

Children learn patterns of behaviors by observing adult models.

Anderson & Faust

Imagine a small child playing with a doll, feeding it and cuddling it. Imagine another child dressing up in western clothes and pretending to be the "cowpoke." Or, imagine two children with toy guns in their hands playing "cops and robbers." No one *taught* these children to behave that way. Instead they learned by observing others, imitating their behaviors. Teachers foster this learning when they say to their students "Watch me do the problem first, then you try it." or "Listen to me read a paragraph, then you read the next one."

Here are some more examples of what we're talking about.

FINISHED PRODUCT
• Give students a chance to preview a completed product—one that is worthy of an "A" grade--before they begin their own (book report, art project, note cards, bibliography, letter, etc.).

PROCESS
• Motor skills are easy to demonstrate either with moving representations, pictures or diagrams.
• To demonstrate how secondary colors are formed from primary colors, put watercolor drops on a transparency on the overhead projector; let the molecules bond together and form the new color.

BEHAVIOR STANDARDS
• In teaching routines for the classroom (sharpening pencils, lining up, clean-up procedures, etc.) role play what they should look like.
• Role play social skills: encouraging others, answering a phone politely, listening, disagreeing in a nice way, etc.

CRITICAL ATTRIBUTES
Although it may be difficult to model every step on a task analysis, try to model or visually demonstrate the critical attribute, rule or generalization:
• To teach that contractions are two words joined together with one or more letters removed and replaced by an apostrophe, have students hold the individual letters while a

child with the apostrophe card bumps out letters to be omitted and takes their place!

• In a geography lesson students are given a three-dimensional world map, blindfolded and told to find a mountain range, peninsula and island by *feeling*.

EXPERIENCES OF PROCESS
• Organize a democratic form of government for the classroom.

• Dramatize the events leading up to the Revolution.

• Take a field trip to the post office, city government, bank, beach, etc.

There is a strong research base supporting the use of concrete materials and visual-spatial activities during instruction (Gagne´, 1985). You've at least doubled the odds that students will remember the information when you provide information both verbally and via visual-spatial means. Just think, if you lose one memory trace, another is still available! Some theorists go beyond this "dual-coding" of information and describe long-term memory as consisting of three parts: episodic, semantic, and procedural memory (Sylwester, 1995). Episodic memory is where your learners will store that field trip experience or the role play. Semantic memory stores the verbal information acquired through reading and lecture—and "drill & kill" worksheets. Procedural memory is our "how to" memory for tasks like typing or riding a bike. Context rich episodic memories are easiest to recall.

Meaning
"Make it meaningful...make it meaningful... make it meaningful...."
We wonder how many teachers are admonished to make their teaching meaningful yet were never really taught *how*. What is it that a teacher can do to make material meaningful and

therefore better remembered? The strategies used to create meaning include:

    1. association (vs. nonsense)
    2. patterned material (vs. unorganized
        material)

    These two categories will make more sense with a brief description of information processing theory. *Information processing theory* is the description of how information entering the brain is processed; that is, what actually happens with the information we presented verbally, visually—with multiple modalities. When we acquire this information, it goes first to our *sensory register.* The learner *perceives* the teacher perhaps writing on the chalkboard while explaining a new concept. Many bits of information are contained in these perceptions—what the teacher is wearing, tone of voice, what's on the chalkboard already, how the learner is feeling at the time...and so on! These sensory perceptions, however, just last a few seconds.

    The learner can actively attend to only a few of these items at a time. What the learner actually concentrates on is held in *short-term memory.* Our *first* problem as teachers is getting the learners to *attend!* Be sure to read the next chapter on motivation because that chapter describes things we can do to help students attend: from dropping our voice to a whisper to using a student's name!

    The information selected for short-term or *working memory* is also of a short duration, probably a matter of seconds. Learners will experience an even quicker decay of the memory trace if the material is nonsense to them (Gage & Berliner, 1984). This explains that first variety of meaningfulness, *association (vs. nonsense):*

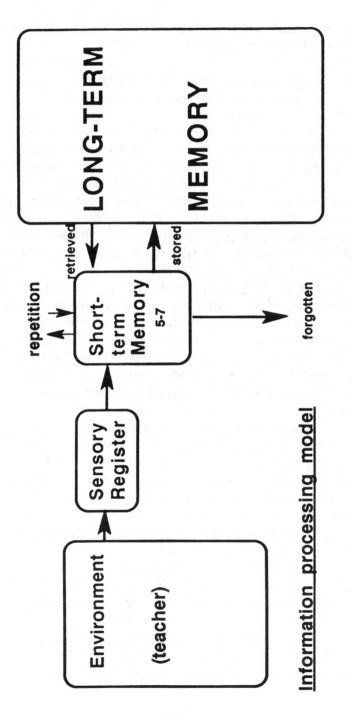

Information processing model

Taking unfamiliar material and associating it by comparing or contrasting, by analogy, and by showing logical relationships to previously stored information aids retention of that new material.

Association

Do we teach nonsense in school? Think of the terminology we use with first graders: noun, vowel, consonant, subtraction; with fourth graders: perimeter, society, long division; with seventh graders: subordinating conjunction, concept; at high school: algorithm, polynomial, postulates.

The teacher has two choices to make:

•to eliminate the unfamiliar word ("nonsense") and substitute familiar words

•or, to use the unknown word (or material) and immediately associate it with the known or familiar

An example of the first choice happened when a second grade teacher asked his class, "Do you understand the *concept* of family?" When he received many blank stares after the question, he rephrased the question, "What does the *word* family mean?" Lots of hands went up!

An example of making an association to something the learner is familiar with would be: "We'll learn about the combining form of 'cide' today. You know the word homicide refers to the killing of a person by another human being. 'Cide' means to kill."

Teachers build these associations when they say:

"*Pulse*...think of the beating of a drum."

"*Subtraction* is just like asking how many baseball cards you'd have left if your friend took some away."

"*Bursa*...it's like a purse and it even sounds like purse!"

The teacher considers the lives of the students. What do they like to listen to, classical music or rock? What do they like to do, skateboard or bicycle? What sports are they familiar with, football or rugby? Knowing this can help in building bridges that will touch the students' lives. Collect this information from your students the first week of school.

All About ME!

1. My favorite television program is....
2. On Saturdays I like to....
3. If I had $10, I would spend it on....
4. My best vacation was....
5. I have been to the following states/countries....
6. The most recent book I read was....

A word of caution is in order. Many times the teacher tries to make an association for the student and the association only makes the learning more confusing:

"Skimming for information is just like skimming the cream off a bottle of milk." (For kids today?)

A logical place to make an association for learners is at the beginning of a lesson, comparing what students are to learn with other learnings, already in long-term memory. Comparing and contrasting similar material will also prevent one from interfering with the other.

"As we work with suffixes today, you'll see that they are similar to prefixes, a small syllable added to a root word. However, suffixes are found in a different place: at the end of the root word."

"The parts of a letter are a little like a telephone conversation. On the telephone we greet whomever we're calling (Hello, Jill), have a conversation (which is the longest part) and then end or close the conversation. A letter also has a greeting, the conversation (which we call the body) and a closing. You'll just have to remember two other parts...."

Making an explicit comparison first, before going on with the steps of the lesson, may profoundly influence retention. Read the following paragraph only once; cover it up and try to repeat the steps.

"You will be learning the steps in an important procedure to be followed in this class. The procedure is actually quite simple. First you arrange things into different groups. Of course one pile may be sufficient, depending on how much there is to do. If you have to go somewhere else due to lack of facilities that's the next step, otherwise you're pretty well set. It's important not to overdo things. That is, it's better to do too few things at once than too many. In the short run this may not seem to be too important but complications can easily arise. A mistake can be expensive as well. At first the whole procedure will seem complicated. Soon, however, it will become just another facet of life. It is difficult to foresee any end to the necessity for this task in the immediate future, but then one can never tell. After the procedure is completed, one arranges the material into different groups again. Then they can be put into their appropriate places. Eventually they will be used once more and the whole cycle will have to be repeated. However, that's part of life." (Bransford & Johnson, 1972, pp. 717-726)

Did you really try to remember the steps in this important process? How'd you do? Would it have helped if we had prefaced the steps in the procedure by saying the procedure is very similar to the process of doing the *laundry*? Read the paragraph again with this comparison in mind....

Remember, "meaningfulness is best judged by the number of associations or networks possible for a given bit of information" (Gage & Berliner, 1984). You may have to make these hooks or associations for your learners. When you've done this, you've also made it easier for learners to retrieve the material in the future.

Pattern

Let's continue that description of the human memory system. We left off describing short-term memory or working memory as holding any information we're attending to for a brief time. Now we need to know *how much* information will fit in this part of the system before it either disappears or is processed into long-term memory.

Very little!

Most researchers describe the storage capacity as somewhere between *five and seven bits of information* (Gagne´, 1985). The bits of information we present in our lesson can be the equivalent, however, of five to seven *pennies* OR five to seven *gold* coins! Study the following list for a few minutes:

limbic system	geography	association
analogy	organize	practice
cerebral cortex	modeling	multiple modalities
meaning	l/r hemisphere	short-term memory
strategies	brain	information processing
processing	comparison	long-term memory
retention	sensory register	reptilian complex

There are 21 bits of information here, too many to memorize easily. Be a good sport, though! Write down as many items as you can remember.

Now study the following list for the same length of time. Sure, it will be easier because they are the same words; but, see how much easier it is to study when the words are organized. After studying the list, try to reproduce it on a piece of scratch paper.

RETENTION

Geography (of brain)	Information processing
cerebral cortex	sensory register
limbic system	short-term memory
reptilian complex	long-term memory
l/r hemisphere	

Strategies
    modeling—multiple
        modalities
    meaning
        association
        comparison
        analogy
        organization
    processing
    practice

Much easier? It should be. The information has been chunked into three major topics with a title. You can easily fit that into your working memory. Taking randomness and changing to orderliness will pay off with faster learning and easier recall.

There are many ways of providing more organization and structure to a lesson:

• State your objective or expectations at the beginning of your lesson. (Remember, though, to keep it in language *meaningful* to your learners.) *"By the end of our lesson today, you'll be able to find a special pattern, sol mi do, in any song as well as write it yourself."*

• When moving from one point to another, announce that you are doing so. *"That's it for the causes of World War I, now for the major events."*

• Give students a list of unit objectives and continually refer back to the list when introducing a new objective.

• Summarize one point before moving on to the next. *"We've just learned that Haiku is a form of poetry whose three lines have a 5-7-5 syllable pattern. Now let's examine common themes in Haiku."*

• Provide a visual organizer or outline for your lesson. *"Here's an outline of the major nutrients we'll study; you fill in additional information as I teach."*

Processing

The message from cognitive researchers this past decade has been that learning is *active* not *passive*! The teacher is no longer viewed as primarily responsible for the dissemination of information. It's not enough merely to provide meaning, modelling and multiple-modality experiences for students. "Without taking away from the important role played by the teacher, it is helpful to remember that what the student does is actually more important in determining what is learned than what the teacher does" (Shuell, 1986). We need to provide opportunities for students to be active in the learning, to construct their own meaning, to *process* what has been taught!

Try the following experiment for a better understanding of processing.

Read the following sentences 3 times. Then, rate each sentence for its pronouncability: + for easy; ~ for moderate; - for somewhat difficult.

1.____The small size of some horse-like animals was caused by poor feed.

2.____Low temperatures alone do little damage to certain plants.

3.____All bodies moving around the sun, such as the earth and moon, cast long shadows into space.

Now, read the next three sentences. Rate each sentence for its ability to provoke a visual image in your mind: + for very vivid; ~ for somewhat vivid; - for no image.

     1.____The earth's crust is broken into 6 major pieces or plates.

     2.____It would take a million atoms side by side to equal the thickness of a piece of paper.

     3.____The largest trees in the world, the redwoods, are cone bearers.

     The last part of this exercise is to try to recall without looking back, the six sentences you've just read. Do the best you can—don't worry about exact wording. First write the sentences you read three times and rated for pronouncability:

1.

2.

3.

Try to remember the three sentences you rated for ability to form a mental image:

1.

2.

3.

     Did you do a better job on those sentences you read with the idea of constructing a visual image? You probably followed the *"law of least effort"* with the tasks: you put no more effort into the task than it required. Because the first three sentences required only reading and pronunciation, that's all you did. The next three sentences required you to do something with the information: to *process*.

You're most likely to remember something you *process*.

Information is likely to remain *inert* if it's not processed. That is, what if the directions for the first three sentences had been to memorize them (not just read them for pronouncability)? The information would have been of little use for problem solving. "Studies show that information that is merely memorized will remain inert even though it is relevant in new situations" (Bransford & Vye, 1989).

So what strategies will invite students to process, particularly when they'd rather follow that "*law of least effort*"?

Processing Strategies
develop questions
give summary
relate to own experience
predict next event
compose a metaphor/analogy
make an inference
image
draw pictures
outline
map
say in own words/retell
evaluate

Ask your students to:
"Jot down two test questions about what you just learned."
"Turn to your study partner and give a summary of the last ten minutes of our lesson."
"As you read, write a one sentence summary for each page."
"Give me at least one example from your own experience when this will apply."
"Let's stop here. Write a prediction of what you think will happen next."
"Compare this to yesterday's lesson. How are they alike?
"Why did this happen? Generate possibilities in your team."

"Form a mental image of what you think that must have looked like."

"Draw a picture of what you think it must have looked like."

"Make a simple outline of what you just heard me say."

"I'll give you an outline of the major topics, you fill in relevant details as we go along."

"Work with another person and make a mind map of how these ideas relate to one another."

"Give me that definition back in different words."

"Debate this issue with your study partner. One be against the issue, the other for it."

Don't forget, if you're going to ask students to map or outline, they need to be taught *how!* In fact, we'd recommend that learners be taught at least three ways of visually processing information (besides outlining):

1. *spider mapping* (to describe a particular topic)

2. *chaining* (to show a process or sequence of events)

3. concept heirarchy (to demonstrate how one concept relates to others)

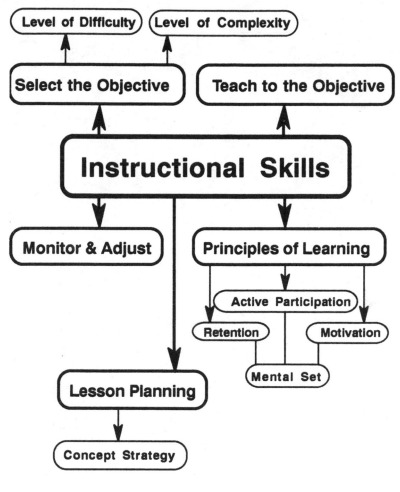

MAP

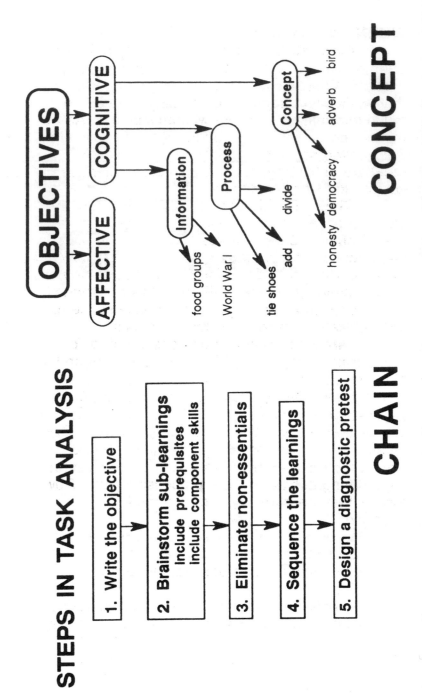

STEPS IN TASK ANALYSIS

1. Write the objective

2. Brainstorm sub-learnings
   Include prerequisites
   Include component skills

3. Eliminate non-essentials

4. Sequence the learnings

5. Design a diagnostic pretest

CHAIN

OBJECTIVES

AFFECTIVE

COGNITIVE

Information

Process

Concept

food groups

World War I

tie shoes

add

divide

honesty democracy

adverb

bird

CONCEPT

WHEN to Process

Amount. Our short-term memory (STM) is often described as the bottleneck of the memory system. While we're capable of learning far more than we'll ever attempt, we can only "take in" so much information at a time without losing it. As we mentioned earlier, that capacity is five to seven bits. This limited capacity of the STM becomes the measure of how much information to present before we provide processing time.

Time. Besides amount of information, the element of time must also be considered. Gagne´ (1985) suggests that it takes 10 seconds to encode each new bit of information. She argues that lectures average 150 words per minute, with about thirty bits of information per minute! If these bits of information are new to students and they try to process them, they're likely to need a full minute for six!

Are we providing the necessary time for processing? Mary Budd Rowe (1983) designed a study to provide the necessary processing time for high school science students. The teachers were required to provide time for students to process the information every 8-12 minutes in the lecture. Two minutes of processing time was given. Students were directed to compare their notes and fill in any gaps during this two minute processing time. Rowe argues that the gaps occur during the lecture because:

1. Short-term memory is simply overloaded.
2. The learner is unclear about an idea presented, tries to interpret it, yet the lecture is continuing.
3. There is an inconsistency between symbols the teacher uses with what the learner read in the text.

4. A point in the lecture sets off a related chain of thoughts that the listener pursues while the teacher continues on!

What did Rowe find when students had these processing opportunities? Students not only remembered more information, but they were able to stay focused for a longer period of time. Remember, though, Rowe researched processing time for high school students with very difficult content. You'll have to be your own researcher, adapting processing time to both the age of your students and the difficulty of the material.

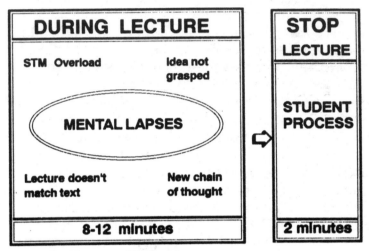

Check Yourself Out!

To help you process the information on modeling/multiple modalities, meaning, and processing, read the following transcript from a science lesson and try to label evidence of the teacher's use of retention theory.

Label each example with
    1. modeling/multiple modalities
    2. meaning
    3. processing

Modeling...people do learn how to behave by watching others.

1._____"Today we'll work on objective #5 on your list. You'll be able to label the parts of a bone."

2._____"The center or shaft of the bone is called the diaphysis. Remember dia from diameter—meaning across the middle."

3._____"When the joint is inflamed, it's called arthritis; tonsils inflamed, tonsilitis; bursa inflamed, bursitis."

4._____Teacher draws a joint on the board, using various colors of chalk to illustrate different parts.

5._____"What could happen when you jump and your bones ram together?" (He actually jumps and then shows his two fists ramming together to illustrate.) "To keep them from splintering, a soft, cushiony, articular cartilege covers the ends of each bone."

6._____Teacher takes out a skeleton. "Now, I'll point to parts of the bone, you write down as many things as you can remember about that part, including the name!"

7._____"The two pads at the knee joint are filled with a fluid: synovial fluid. This fluid must be kept clean for the joint to work properly. If it's not, you'll have this done." (He takes out a syringe, role plays taking fluid out of knee cap. Kids moan and groan!)

8._____"Imagine yourself falling out of a tree and landing on your knees; what do you think will happen? See if the person sitting next to you agrees with your thoughts."

Check your answers:
1. meaning (organization)
2. meaning (building bridge/hook from nonsense)
3. meaning (logical relationship)
4. modeling (visual diagram/colored chalk)

5. modeling—multiple modalities (showing process by jumping)
6. modeling (skeleton); processing (writing)
7. modeling—multiple modalities (role play)
8. processing

How'd you do? Is it worth the extra effort? You bet! The greater the strength of the original learning, the less forgetting the students will experience. We can't stop here, though, just getting the information logged into memory. Learners need to be able to retrieve that information a day from now, a week from now, even one month from now. What can you do to make this a reality? Provide....

Practice
Original learning + <u>Practice</u> = Retention

Does practice make perfect? The only practice that makes perfect is perfect practice! What does that mean? That means we need to design the most effective practice sessions possible if we are to increase retention. Just providing opportunity to practice is not enough. We need to consider:
Amount of material: whole or part?
Amount of time: long or short?
When: spaced or massed?
How?
Feedback

Amount of material: Whole or Part?
The argument over whether whole or part learning is better has been going on for a long time! Gestaltists feel one needs to gain a "feel" for the whole first—to "size up" overall meaning. Others feel it's easier for the learner to start with a small piece at a time. It looks like we've finally reached a compromise.

Allow learners to experience the integrated whole *first* and then practice parts! In deciding what constitutes a "part," find a relatively complete section of the learning that retains meaning. For instance, let's assume you're going to teach students to sing all four verses of "America the Beautiful." You'd want to break it down into smaller "chunks," maybe starting with only half the first verse. Just remember that those small chunks have to be *meaningful*. Or you demonstrate the process of long division, then announce that students will learn and practice the skill of estimating first.

Here's another example. In a beginning class in keyboarding, we normally start with the "home row": a,s,d,f,j,k,l ;. That gives a key for each finger and still allows for the "construction" of a few words in that initial lesson: sad, lad, fad....to list a few. It's a small part of the keyboard (part, NOT whole) and is meaningful (words, not random letters).   Remember, though, that part practice is better early in the learning, while the whole method is better later.

Other motor activities are so closely knit that they cannot be broken into parts...like the swan dive. These activities must be practiced as a whole.

Amount of Time: Long or Short?

Practice periods during the initial learning should be relatively short. Many short practice opportunities are more effective than one or two long ones. Why? Because with longer practice periods we begin to get bored and lose interest! Have you ever watched students who were told: "Take the next 40 minutes and review your notes for tomorrow's test." What do these kids look like 15 minutes into the review? Looking around...chatting...taking a bathroom break.... Then, have you ever heard a teacher say:

"Let's keep it quiet. Others are trying to study."

Wouldn't it be much more productive (for you and your students!) to take that 40 minutes and distribute it over 4 days—10 minutes of review time each day before the test. Or even two 20-minute review sessions are less likely to create the boredom.

When: Spaced or Massed?

Notice, we still asked students to practice 40 minutes, but spaced the sessions over a period of time. *Spaced* practice over several lessons is superior to *massing* the practice—perhaps in one long session (Walberg, 1988). How superior? According to Walberg, probably *twice* as effective as massed practice! That sure seems to explain why those of us who crammed for exams remembered very little of that information after a period of time.

Distributing the practice periods will assist us with another memory phenomenon: the brain remembers best that which came first and that which came last. If you try to study one hour straight, you'll only have one "primacy" and one "recency" effect. Yet, if that hour is broken into three 20-minute reviews, you'll have six!

Buzan (1984) suggests a structure for distributing practice periods: "1...1...1...4." That is, one day later, one week later, one month later, and four months later.   This is assuming, of course, that learners had processing time during initial instruction. He would suggest processing (or practice) time after every ten minute period of instruction.

Don't stop providing practice for your students just because they've mastered the material. "*Overlearning*" is one of the best assists to both retention of information and truly understanding the material!

How?

Reviews (practice) are not repetitions per se. Don't ask students to read or listen or watch just *one more time*! Unfortunately, if you asked some students how they plan to study for the test that's precisely what they'll say:

"I'll read through my notes again."

"I'll read the chapter again."

Reading the material "one more time" is just putting information into short-term memory "one more time" and probably dumping it as it fills up. Worse yet, those learners suffer *delusions of familiarity*—"Oh, yeah, I read that before." The key to review is to pull the information back out of long-term memory on your own.

Here's an example. The class is preparing for a test on Coastal Indians on Friday. A 12-minute practice session occurs at the beginning of class each day:

Monday: Describe the living conditions of Coastal Indians. Then compare your answers with the text's. What did you leave out?

Tuesday: How are the Coastal Indians like the Plateau Indians we studied last week? Unlike? Compare your description with your teammates. What did your teammate have that you didn't?

Wednesday: Brainstorm everything you can remember about Coastal Indians. Count your 'ideas'.

Thursday: Review the chapter on Coastal Indians. In your team, make a spider map showing religion, food, and transportation on chart paper. Use lots of colors!

Friday: Test

Each review session required students to structure the answers—to think.

Time for practice doesn't come just from class time. Think about homework as an opportunity for practice. Homework (particularly when it is graded or commented on) raises learning from the 50th to the 79th percentile (Walbert, Paschal, & Weinstein, 1985). It's such a missed opportunity for practice time—especially in light of the statistics: high school students average only 4-5 hours a week for homework yet 28 hours a week of television.

CAUTION: Don't fall into the trap of doing the reviewing for your students! Most of us have heard a teacher say, "Let me go over this one more time...."

Who's getting the most benefit from the review? The teacher, of course! The kids are probably suffering from more *delusions of familiarity.* This type of review is perhaps more effective if the learners are first asked to remember the information on their own—before the teacher fills in the gaps. For the best practice, someone (author unknown) once said,

> *Let the teacher do the inspiring,*
> *Let the students do the perspiring!*

Feedback

On a piece of scratch paper practice making a line 2.5 centimeters long. Now, keep practicing for about five minutes.

We doubt you actually practiced for five minutes. You probably said to yourself, "This is ridiculous. How do I know if I'm right?" The same is true for most practice. How can one improve without knowing a mistake was made, what it was, and how to corrrect it?

With short practice periods, feedback may be given on a small "chunk" before a new learning is added. This helps the learner to really zero in on what needs to be practiced.

Most coaches can relate to this. Assume that a player is not doing a good job of blocking. The coach helps the student by breaking the process down into smaller parts and concentrating on the part that really needs to be improved. The coach doesn't say, "You're just not blocking." Instead, the coach might say: "You've got to keep your head up, not down; otherwise you can't see your target." The feedback is specific, immediate, and concentrating on the small part that must be practiced to improve the player's blocking ability.

Practice with immediate feedback is most important for skill development, procedural knowledge, or concept development. When practicing declarative knowledge (names, dates, facts, etc.), it's more important to try to integrate or organize it with other information we have in long-term memory.

Check Yourself Out!

O.K.—let's practice what we're preaching. Let's say you find the information in this book helpful (and we hope you do). How should you review or practice it in the future?

Amount
How much of the book should you review? How much time will you spend?

When will you begin? **When** will you schedule review sessions?

How will you actually construct your review session?

Feedback: If your goal is to remember the information, how will you check yourself?

If your goal is to practice the strategies (procedures) recommended, how will you know how well you're doing?

Summary

Understanding our wonderful three-pound brain helps us better understand how our students remember information. The capacity for remembering is there. The question is, are we tapping it?

For of all sad words of tongue or pen,
The saddest are these: "It might have been!"
J. G. Whittier

Brain research helps us understand why certain strategies work to aid retention. We know that the degree of the original learning is improved when

Models are provided.
There are many paths to learning
That don't require words. *

Multiple-modality experiences are included.
There is nothing so unequal
As the equal treatment of unequals. *

Meaning is provided through organization and associations or hooks.
The least of things with a meaning is worth more in life
than the greatest of things without it.
C.G. Jung

Students are given opportunity to process the information.

Learning without thought is labor lost;
thought without learning is perilous.
Confucius

A minute of thought is worth more
than an hour of talk. *

Effective practice or review sessions are provided.

Practice is the best of all instructors.
Publilius Syrus

No one knows what he can do till he tries.
Publilius Syrus

*authors unknown

Chapter 7

Motivation

Can you:
- **describe "success x value" theory**
- **relate attributions to expectations for success**
- **give examples of**
  insuring success
  helping students link effort to success
  appropriate level of concern
- **describe techniques to motivate using feeling tone, interest, knowledge of results, and extrinsic rewards**

"I don't see why we have to learn that."
"I don't want to do it."
"This stuff is boring."
Kids aren't passive receivers of information; they choose what they want to attend to. The same student who may have uttered one of the comments above may leave class and be highly motivated to play video games or shoot baskets. Motivation has both direction and intensity. That is, a student may direct attention to both video games and shooting baskets, but with varying degrees of effort. Our dilemma as teachers is to get students to direct their efforts toward school tasks with an acceptable degree of effort.

How do we do it? There's an old story of the man who bought a mule because it was supposed to be so smart. After getting the mule home and not being able to get it to do anything, he returned to the farmer from whom he'd purchased it. After listening to the man's complaints about the mule not doing anything, the farmer said: "I'll fix that." He promptly picked up a 2x4 and whammed the mule on the head. "Gotta get his attention before you can get him to do anything!"

Does this happen in the classroom? Let's see:

Student: "I don't see why we have to learn that."
Teacher: "Well, if you want a passing grade in this class...."

Student: "This stuff is boring."
Teacher: "I've taken about all I'm going to from you today; go to the office!"

Threats, shame, punishment...poor motivators for students. Schools assume built-in motivation but when it does not occur, coercion is used—which creates the very discipline problems they were trying to prevent! (Glasser, 1990). Anxiety is one way to motivate students, but it's not the only way. In fact, the unpleasant feelings that such techniques generate may last "three seconds to a lifetime." Is it worth it?

"If they'd only try. I know they can do it." Oh, but do the *students* know they can do it? Do they value the task itself or the rewards it will bring? The amount of effort a student puts into a task is a function both of how successful the student expects to be and the value placed on the task. This theory (Brophy, 1987) is often expressed as

Effort = success x value

For example, a student may love to play football and will try out for the school football team *if* that student believes there is a chance of making it. But, if one of these conditions is missing, no effort will be put forth to try out for the team. If the student believes the competition is so great there's no chance of getting on the team—why try out? Loving to play football isn't enough.

Expectations for Success

Let's examine the first element in the equation: *expectations for success.*

If a student feels that she has no control over her success, she is unlikely to exert any effort. Lack of success may be blamed on the teacher, the difficulty of the task, or one's own ability, or just plain bad luck. Similarly, the student may believe that success is due to good luck, an easy task, or to innate ability. The ideal situation would be if the student attributes success or failure to her own effort. That places the student *in control* and increases the likelihood that she will work hard to satisfy her need to succeed.

Notice the possible combinations on the following chart. Of the *internal* attributions (ability and effort), the student only has control over effort. Effort is subject to change. If a student *believes* that her effort will change the outcome in a class, she is more likely to study!

Ability is considered a stable characteristic. Students expect the future to be a mirror image of the past. This is particularly problematic when they believe they are not capable in a particular subject and their belief is inaccurate. Why put any effort into a class if the results will remain the same?

With the *external* attributions, the learner believes she is merely a pawn, not in control of her own destiny. The result of this belief, however, is the same as the belief that one does not have the ability to succeed: Why bother trying if it won't make a difference?

ATTRIBUTIONS

INTERNAL	ABILITY	EFFORT
Success	I'm capable.	I really tried.
Failure	I'm not smart.	I didn't try.
EXTERNAL	TASK DIFFICULTY	LUCK
Success	It was so easy!	I'm lucky!
Failure	It was too hard.	Rotten luck.

Adapted from Weiner, 1979.

Do you have any control over these expectations? You bet! You can't afford to have your students operating on a negative self-fulfilling prophecy. If they believe they have no control or don't believe in their own ability, of course they won't try. You *can* break this pattern by:

- designing instruction to insure success, and
- teaching students to take responsibility for their own success or failure.

Insuring Success

The better you are at predicting the correct level of difficulty for a student, the more likely you'll help that learner *feel* successful. Note the word FEEL. Just because you are successful in completing a task does not mean you *feel* successful. Suppose you were asked to practice tying your shoe for the next ten minutes. You will probably be successful but not feel successful. If the probability of being successful is either too high or too low, minimal effort will be put forth. Our job as teachers is to diagnose our learners to find out where their old learning leaves off and new learning begins.

Remember Chapter 2, writing task analyses and conducting a diagnostic survey?

Do you give your students any assignments that aren't due for a long period of time? If so, why not break that assignment into smaller steps, each step due in short periods of time--not "three weeks from now." Some students don't even try when the assignment seems massive or too far into the future. Instead of assigning a research report that will be due in three weeks, try

	Due	Points
Topic	Day 2	5
Sources	Day 4	10
Notecards	Day 8	15
Outline	Day 10	15
Visuals	Day 12	10
Rough draft	Day 15	15
Title page, bibliography	Day 17	5
Final report	Day 21	20

The closer the goal, the more likely we'll try. Setting daily goals for students (and helping students set daily goals) gives them a chance to experience success from mastery of one task and that feeling is likely to motivate the student to begin the next! It's much better to set a goal to get one more problem correct tomorrow than to state a global goal of "doing a better job."

Another way to assist students in daily goal setting is to require that they keep an assignment sheet to record all assignments (goals). Have them check off an assignment when it is complete and record points earned. This helps them see the relationship between effort and outcomes! They know on a daily basis where they stand "grade-wise".

Successful experiences in school are likely to result in a positive academic self concept. The individual strives desperately to secure some assurance of his self worth....

B. Bloom

Assignment sheet: Math				
Due	Assignment	✓	points	total points

Don't forget make-up tests. That feeling of "all or nothing" that some students have on a test is likely to contribute to a poor performance or worse yet, giving up without even trying. If students know they will have the opportunity to take the test over again, another chance to be successful, they may exert more effort.

You may have to vary the standard of performance for some students. In a lesson on paragraph development, some students may be required to write one paragraph, others to work on three.

Clear direction-giving can't be emphasized enough! Giving clear and precise directions can increase the learner's chances of being successful on a task. Have you ever wondered how many students experienced failure because they didn't understand the directions? Think through your directions first:

•If there are 3 steps or more, put them in writing.
•Write them in a sequential format, numbering the steps.
•Prepare a visual model of the completed product.
•Decide how you will check student understanding
 before they practice independently.

Don't forget that some students will just require more instructional time! If we believe that all students can learn, given the time and help they need, the question is "What **can** I do?" instead of "What can **I** do?"

> •Try to find some extra minutes to provide instruction to those students needing it (pulling them aside while others work independently; as you monitor individuals).
> •Provide alternative styles of instruction like additional texts, films, self-instructional programs, audio-cassettes of the textbook.
> •Cooperative team learning is one form of providing additional instructional time as students help one another in teams and manage to explain concepts in a language more readily understood by other students.

Knowledge of Results (and, teaching students to take responsibility for success or failure)

Students show up in class with either internal or external attributions of their success or failure. These feelings about themselves will determine how much effort they put into your class. If they believe they have low ability, they fail to exert effort in class. "Why try, I'll fail anyway." In the last section we examined how you can build in successful experiences for students; now we'll look at changing student attributions through feedback or knowledge of results. We'll begin first with a focus on knowledge of results in general, something we all need to motivate us. Then, we'll look at tailoring the knowledge of results for those students with external attributions; they see no relationship between their effort and their success or failure. When we provide knowledge of results on their work, we want them to see the relationship between the amount of effort they put into the task and the results.

Do you check student work promptly? Do your students have ways to get feedback about whether their answers are right or wrong? Can your students check their own work immediately, perhaps even recording their own score? If you answered yes to these questions, you're doing a great job motivating your students with the learning principle KNOWLEDGE OF RESULTS. Knowledge of results means providing your students with information about the adequacy of their responses. To be of maximum value, knowledge of results must be

> 1. immediate (Challenge yourself— provide knowledge of correctness of responses within **one hour**.)
> 2. specific

The reinforcement a student experiences when finding out if an answer is correct contributes to the feeling of success we've been talking about. The corrective nature of the feedback to an answer that is wrong also contributes to keeping focus on the learning.

Dealing with unsatisfactory student responses is tough for all of us. But, we have to deal with them. It is better to tell a student the answer is wrong than to ignore the answer. And, it is even better to provide the correct response than simply say the answer is wrong.

There is a danger that if you always provide the right answer, kids will get lazy or careless and pay less attention. To avoid this very possible situation, anticipate it! Get evidence from the student that she can make the correction without your assistance, before letting the student move on. "You solve the next problem while I stand and watch," or "See if you can paraphrase what I just said."

Now for some specific examples of providing immediate and specific knowledge of results:

> • Don't just assign a grade for a writing assignment; explain the grade: "You did a fine job of developing the story elements of initial incident and rising action. You need to include falling action at the end."

• Students can correct their own papers...unless it's a big exam and you're uneasy! (You will still need to monitor these papers to be sure errors were detected.)
• Even if it's a quiz, collect the papers and read the answers.
• Send home a partial answer sheet with the homework (answers to odd number problems in math, still requiring students to show work).
• Set up an "answer corner" in the room with teacher manual or answer sheet available; students having difficulty may refer to these for assistance.
• When reports are due regularly, assign each row a different day of the week as "due date"; you are able to correct Monday's row the same day (and you save ruining your weekend with 30 some papers to correct!).

Prepare scales for any assignments you give that will require additional time to correct. You can cut down on the time it takes to write long comments and add to the specificity of the feedback. For example, in written composition:

	LOW			HIGH
handwriting	1	2	3	4
spelling	1	2	3	4
punctuation	1	2	3	4
word usage	1	2	3	4
organization	2	4	6	8
ideas	2	4	6	8

(adapted from Diedrich, French & Carlton)

Specific feedback provided by the Diedrich scale tells a student what to fine tune the next time written composition is assigned. Just receiving an "A" or a "C" on a paper is likely to encourage a student to use external attributions: "The teacher liked my paper!" or "The teacher must have been in a bad mood!"

In developing your scales, capitalize on the need to assist some students in seeing the relationship between their effort and success by having them do a self-estimate of their own points. This requires the student to look at what they did and place a point value on *their effort*. They are in control of their own success!

Social studies report: grading scale	points	self estim.	final points
Title page	5		
Biography note			
quality, completeness	20		
note construction	20		
bibliography	5		
handwriting	5		
Map			
completeness	20		
accuracy, neatness	10		
Opinion note			
validity	15		
paragraph construction	10		
handwriting	5		

Primary students gain ownership of their success in printing with the following scale:

MY PRINTING		
yes	**no**	
		I printed from left to right. **go ⟶ stop**
		I made straight sticks. **I**
		I made round balls. **O**
		I made the letters touch the ceiling and floor.
		I made finger spaces between words. **is** **good**
		I pressed lightly.
		I did beautiful work. ☺ **I tried hard.** 😐 **I raced.**

In spelling, help your learners see their success by recording both the self-corrected pretest and the final test.

Words correct

Lesson #1	1	2	3	4	5	6	7	8	9
pretest	▓	▓	▓	▓					
posttest	█	█	█	█	█	█	█	█	

As we assist students in keeping track of the progress, help them make goal statements. Model high expectations for them: "I know you can improve in the posttest. We'll take 10 minutes each day and practice to make sure that happens!" Help them attribute their problems to their own lack of effort: "Last week you had 9 correct and you spent time each day studying. That's why you did so well! Let's look at what happened this week." We want students to see that hard work pays off and not blame failure on either low ability or bad luck.

If you want learners to have ownership for their success or failure, you must give them ownership! That is, when you preface your feedback with the words

"I really like...."

you are directing student attention to YOU, not what they did! Try taking those words out of your feedback and replace them with "You...."

"*You* really used your time wisely on this project and your grade reflects it."

"*You* must feel really proud of that report." Listen carefully to student reactions to success or failure. When they attribute success to their effort, reinforce them, "Yes, and that effort really paid off!" If they attribute failure to lack of effort, again, reinforce that belief, "Yes, if you had spent more time in preparing for it, I know you would have done better."

Provide feedback forms to students requiring goal statements like:

I did well on _____
Next time I will improve by_____

Remember, though, kids have to believe they have a chance at success if they put forth the effort. How would you like to confront the following chart every day in your classroom:

SPELLING PROGRESS					
Test #	1	2	3	4	5
Sid	75	90	90	85	100
Kent	40	45	40	abs.	abs.
Natasha	100	100	95	100	95

Any wonder why Kent was absent the last two weeks? Is the following chart any better?

Bookworms	
Jason	★★★★★★★★★★★★★★★
Sean	★★★★★★★
Carole	★★

Carole probably decided there was no chance of catching up, so why bother? It's easier on her self concept to say, "I don't like to read so I don't care!" Internally, she might be saying "I'm not as capable as Jason and Sean."

Creating Appropriate Level of Concern

Remember the last time you had to give a speech or make a presentation? Did you get butterflies in your stomach just thinking about it? How about those final exams in college? Now, you didn't spend more time worrying about them than you did studying for them, did you? There is another name for those butterflies and that worry—LEVEL OF CONCERN.

You were worried about how competent you'd look in front of your peers when you gave that speech. You were afraid of failing that college course. Or, maybe you were worried that you'd lose the respect of your professor if you didn't do well. Fear of losing something that you need or want (status, success, esteem, etc.) will MOTIVATE. It's not just that expectation for success that determines our performance on a task, it may be our fear of failure!

Level of concern is just like medication when you're ill. Without it you won't get any better; with too much you'll really be sick. It is only with the *right* dosage that you get well. It's finding the right dosage of level of concern for every student in a classroom that's rough. Remember....

no concern ➝ no motivation for task
some concern ➝ focus on task
too much concern ➝ can't concentrate on task

In the classroom it looks like this:

Teacher: "John, take as much time as you'd like to do your health report. It's not going to be graded, anyway."
　　　　Result: John's not worried about anything now, is he? He has very little concern about the task...and may not even start it. What's there to lose?
Teacher: "John, you'll have one week to finish your health report. I'll be checking with you each day, though, to see how far along you are."
　　　　Result: Level of concern just shot up. Not too high, though. One week is a reasonable length of time. John is "motivated" to work on the report because he doesn't want to lose either the teacher's respect or get a poor grade in the class.
Teacher: "John, get this report done by tomorrow. Whether you pass this class or not is dependent on the grade you get on it."
　　　　Result: Level of concern just shot past the safety zone.

John had planned to go to the football game after school. Now what? He's upset. In fact, more of his energy will be spent on his anger and frustration than on the task itself. Too much concern is interfering with focus on the report.

Did you notice how the teacher could influence level of concern? The teacher can increase concern or can lower it, just as a teacher can influence expectations for success. When might you want to lower level of concern?

- before students have to take part in contests (i.e., athletic, speech, spelling)
- when students have to perform before an audience
- in "test" situations (i.e., quizzes, aptitude /achievement tests, final exams)

Many of the same techniques that were mentioned above for increasing a student's expectations for success can be used to lower anxious feelings:

- Practice beyond the point of mastery. Give that speech many times perfectly before giving it for real. Rehearse that play again and again before the opening curtain.
- Look for evidence of too much stress in problem solving or discovery situations—the two don't mix.
- Give many short quizzes rather than one big exam.
- Offer to do the first problem or two with a student to reduce tension enough so the student can proceed alone.
- Offer a word of encouragement, "Good topic sentence."
- Relaxation exercises can lower stress before an exam!

The situation becomes more complex when we consider the fact that some students have a low level of concern in some of the same situations where other students are highly anxious. If we lower their concern, it will cause a decrease in effort. For these students, we can raise level of concern.

- Give a reminder of how important the task is for a grade.
- Call on non-volunteers to participate.
- Use physical presence—stand beside the student.

Needless to say, the same techniques may be appropriate for creating focus in one student yet raise level of concern too much in another. Skillful teaching will require a balance between maintaining an appropriate level of concern while maintaining success expectations in students. Brophy (1987) lists a supportive environment, without anxiety, and appropriate level of challenge or difficulty as essential preconditions to motivating by maintaining success expectations.

Check Yourself Out!

Let's pause and digest what's been said so far. We've been looking at one side of the equation:

Effort = **expectations for success**   x   task value

In particular, expectations for success can be influenced by
1. insuring success (through task manipulation)
2. providing knowledge of results, and
3. creating appropriate level of concern

List examples of what you can do to insure success on a task:
1.
2.
3.

Now, what can you do to provide immediate and specific knowledge of results:
1.
2.

High levels of concern can evoke responses
incompatible with successful performance.

Anderson & Faust

What additional measures can you take to help
students attribute their success to their own effort:
1.
2.

Incentive Value of the Task

It's time to look at the second factor influencing
the effort students put into a task.

Effort = expectations for success x **task value**

The task may be moderately difficult and the student
may expect to be successful, but if the task has no
value incentive, why do it? We'll divide our
discussion into the following categories:
INTEREST (in the task)
FEELING TONE (while doing the task)
EXTRINSIC REWARDS (for doing the task)
In each, we'll examine what a teacher can do to
stimulate motivation to learn by increasing the value
of the task.

Interest

!TCEPXE T'NSEOD RENRAEL EHT
GNIHTEMOS !TNEREFFID TI EKAM !LEVON TI
EKAM

Did you expect this? Did you experience
increased focus? It is a way to capture interest:
something novel, different. Repeated practice on
math facts or spelling words, or timed writings in
keyboarding can produce negative results—lack of
effort due to habituation. Can you turn that otherwise
boring assignment into a gamelike activity? One
teacher turned his timed writings into a football game
with the class. The class was divided into two teams.
Daily he'd draw a name from each team, using their

words per minute as number of yards traveled on a football field he'd created on a bulletin board!

Interest is also created when a task relates to the student personally. When constructing worksheets, take time to add student names, the school name, or even popular football teams or music groups. Find out what your students like by conducting an interest survey that first week of school. (See Chapter 6 for an example.)

Give students choices for projects or reports and they're likely to select the one most interesting to them personally and put more effort into it! An English teacher gave her students the following choices for a project on *Romeo and Juliet*:

- Make a calendar or timeline that shows major events.
- Present a short scene using puppets.
- Read *Westside Story*, compare the 2 plays.
- Make a collage that represents your feelings about the play.
- Propose and design your own project!

Goodlad (1984) did not find innovative or enthusiastic learning in his extensive study of schools. He found that teacher talk and monitoring of students took the place of small group activity or activities that allowed students to plan or initiate anything. He concluded that perhaps "teachers teach as they were taught."

Feeling Tone

Don't you work best in an environment that's warm and supportive? So, too, do students. They are more likely to value participation in an activity or put forth effort if there is an absence of criticism or chaos. Yet, the absence of unpleasant feeling tone is not enough. A neutral feeling tone can be downright BORING! Teaching is a little like selling.

Students didn't come to school ready to "buy" lessons on composition or history. We have some selling to do to help establish the value of such information.

Remember the power of modeling we discussed in Chapter 7? Teachers who model an interest in their subject, who model enthusiasm for information are likely to have students who are more task oriented (Bettencourt et al.,1983). They're more likely to "sell' students on the lesson! Ask any principal or teacher to describe the attributes of an effective teacher and the answer will probably include "teacher enthusiasm."

What are the indicators of enthusiasm? Collins (1978) identified eight: rapid, uplifting vocal delivery; dancing, wide open eyes; frequent, demonstrative gestures; varied, dramatic body movements; varied emotive facial expressions; selection of varied words, especially adjectives; ready, animated acceptance of ideas and feelings; and exuberant overall energy level. A great way to find out how you rate on the enthusiasm scale is to videotape yourself teaching. (It's not as painful as it sounds, and no one else has to look at it!)

Just think, enthusiasm is a teachable skill! Do we need more of it in schools? You bet. Goodlad (1984) found very little affect—either positive or negative—in classrooms. He suggests that the boredom students feel with school may be a result of the "flat, neutral emotional ambiance of most of the classes we studied."

Extrinsic Rewards

What motivated you to read this book? Do you have a burning desire to learn as much as you can about the science of teaching? Or was it a professor or maybe even a principal who strongly suggested you read it? When you are motivated to do something simply for the love of doing it, we label that motivation INTRINSIC. There is no apparent reward. When you are motivated because of the payoff you will receive, which is not related to the task at all, we call it EXTRINSIC. This could be a better grade in a course or a better evaluation from a principal.

When you capitalize on student interests or your enthusiasm creates a stimulating environment, you are enhancing intrinsic motivation. Yet, it's difficult to arouse curiosity or turn lessons into game-like activities for everything we teach. Yes, we will have to use extrinsic incentives like praise, feedback, grades, or rewards. We discussed feedback or knowledge of results earlier as it relates to success.

Tangible rewards. You know what these are...stickers, stars, popcorn parties. Students are offered such rewards if they'll read a certain number of books, finish a math paper, or just be a good listener! Of all the motivators, these are perhaps the most difficult to use. There is some evidence that extrinsic rewards may undermine intrinsic motivation under certain conditions (Morgan, 1984; Cameron & Pierce, 1994). How could that be? When students already have an intrinsic liking of a task (i.e., reading books), offering a reward suggests that the activity (reading a book) is not worth doing for its own sake. In fact, if the reward is highly desired by the learners, they may hurry through the task, putting less effort into it, just to get the reward. Remember our students with external attributions? Rewards may foster that feeling of being under the control of external forces, decreasing internal attributions.

Then how do we use rewards effectively? Make sure the reward symbolizes success or mastery of a task. It's not just finishing a math paper; it's improving considerably from the last paper. It's not just counting number of books read; it's carefully reporting the value or contents of each book.

Most of the success stories we've heard about using token economies or contracting for behavior come out of special education classes. The class size smaller, and therefore effective use of rewards is easier. Many times these students have less intrinsic liking of school tasks than in a regular classroom because of lack of success in these classes. Thus, in special education classes there is less risk of undermining intrinsic motivation.

Praise. Verbal praise may actually enhance intrinsic motivation (Cameron & Pierce, 1994). And it's easier to use! Now this is not to suggest massive doses of praise; in fact, it's quality not quantity that counts. What does "quality" praise sound like? Brophy (1981) gives us guidelines:

Effective praise
1. Is delivered contingently.
2. Specifies the particulars of the accomplishment.
3. Shows spontaneity, variety, and other signs of credibility; suggests clear attention to the student's accomplishment.
4. Rewards attainment of specified performance criteria (which can include effort criteria, however).
5. Provides information to students about their competence or the value of their accomplishments.
6. Orients students towards better appreciation of their own task-related behavior and thinking about problem solving.
7. Uses students' own prior accomplishments as the context for describing present accomplishments.
8. Is given in recognition of noteworthy effort or success at difficult task (for *this* student).
9. Attributes success to effort and ability, implying that similar successes can be expected in the future.

10. Focuses students' attention of their own task-relevant behavior.
11. Fosters appreciation of and desirable attributions about task-relevant behavior after the process is completed.

Ineffective praise
1. Is delivered randomly or unsystematically.
2. Is restricted to global positive reactions.
3. Shows a bland uniformity, which suggests a conditioned response made with minimal attention.
4. Rewards mere participation, without consideration of performance processes or outcomes.
5. Provides no information at all or gives students information about their status.
6. Orients students toward comparing themselves with others and thinking about competing.
7. Uses the accomplishments of peers as the context for describing students' present accomplishments.
8. Is given without regard to the effort expended or the meaning of the accomplishment (for *this* student).
9. Attributes success to ability alone or to external factors such as luck or easy task.
10. Focuses students' attention on the teacher as an external authority figure who is manipulating them.
11. Intrudes into the ongoing process, distracting attention from task-relevant behavior.

Wow! We've come full-circle in studying motivation. This chapter began by exploring what you can do to change students' expectations for success; in particular, their attributions. We've ended up with guidelines for effective use of praise; a social reinforcer that adds to the value of the task. Yet, praise, effectively used, helps students link their successes to their effort!

Cooperative Team Learning

Do you know what kids like best about school? Answer: other kids! Why not capitalize on that intrinsic motivation to build in value for school tasks. That is, why not have students work on assignments in a cooperative group setting (instead of alone) and reap the benefits of greater effort being put into the task? Other motivational variables are at work, too, in a group setting. Cooperative learning:

•Insures **success** by providing additional instructional time for those most in need as they are "tutored" by their teammates.

•Provides **immediate knowledge of results,** since students check with peers anytime instead of having to wait on the availability of the teacher.

•Raises **level of concern** appropriately, due to peer expectations.

•Stimulates **interest** through novelty. According to Goodlad (1984), while the opportunity to interact with peers is intrinsically motivating to most students, groupwork was a rarity.

Now just putting kids into teams and saying, "Do the assignment together," is not going to work nor will it have the motivational payoffs described above. You are changing the rules on the kids. They've gone through a school system that repeatedly has told them to "Turn around and do your own work!" and now you are saying the opposite. Effective use of cooperative teams will require the teaching of new routines to students as well as instruction in social skills. (See *Managing a Cooperative Classroom* by Cummings for more information.)

Check Yourself Out!

Before we summarize, why don't you give it a try? Translate the model below into a verbal description of motivation.

Effort =

Expectations for success	x	Task value
insure success		provide interest (self & novelty)
provide knowledge of results (immediate,specific)		provide positive feeling tone (enthusiasm)
maintain appropriate level of concern		use praise effectively

Summary

Yes, teachers can be active participants in increasing the motivation of their students. True, students arrive with their own attributions for success or failure but we can structure the classroom to increase their internal attributions or ownership and get greater expenditure of effort. We can also take advantage of that which intrinsically motivates students to add to the value of the task at hand. The environment we create through our own enthusiasm and effective use of praise can't help but motivate learners.

The mediocre teacher tells
The good teacher explains
The superior teacher demonstrates
The great teacher inspires
Wm. Arthur Ward

Chapter 8

Active Participation

<table>
<tr><td>

Can you:
- give the rationale for active participation
- give examples of active participation
- relate active participation to
     motivation
     congruency

</td></tr>
</table>

"How come you called on me? I didn't raise my hand!" Ever heard that one? There are probably not many teachers who haven't. Remember that human beings follow a psychological principle called *The Law of Least Effort* (and students are no exception): they put no more effort into a task than the task requires! Teachers can't afford to give students that option...sitting in class sleeping with their eyes open. That old saying captures it all:

When I hear, I forget
When I see, I remember
When I do, I learn

To insure learning, we must get students involved!
    Classroom management—i.e., "using questioning and recitation strategies that maintain active participation by all students..." ranks highest out of 28 factors influencing student learning (Wang et al., 1994).
    "...learning from teaching is not automatic. It occurs primarily through *active* and *effortful* information processing by students who must

perceive and interpret teachers' actions for them to influence achievement" (Wittrock, 1986).

The amount of active participation in a class is an index of quality instruction. Yes, even with a group of thirty youngsters, it is possible to get the active involvement of the majority of the class and achieve results that are comparable to that of one-on-one tutoring (Bloom, 1984). The key, however, is not to make participation in class *voluntary*—or we're back to that Law of Least Effort.

As we cited earlier, classrooms have not traditionally provided for active participation by all. Rather, the students in the top third (academically) of classes tend to receive the most encouragement and support for participation while those students in the bottom third are practically ignored. Walberg (1988) calls this the *"Matthew effect"*...the (academically) rich get richer, the poor get poorer.

For unto every one that hath shall be given,
and he shall have abundance;
but from him that hath not
shall be taken away even that which he hath.
Matthew 25:29

When

When do you involve your students? Consistently—not eventually. Students must be consistently involved during all of these activities:

- direct instruction/teacher talk
- whole group discussion
- small group work
- independent work

During Direct Instruction and Discussion

Now is a good time for you to go back and review the Retention chapter, particularly the section on processing. You can deliberately plan opportunities for student participation in the lesson after each step in your task analysis, when their short-term memory has reached its capacity, or when you intuitively sense the need! A real informal rule of thumb has been called *physiological attention span:* one minute per year. Try talking to five year olds for more than five minutes—you may see visible evidence of the need for active participation!

When you're asking those questions to get consistent involvement, don't forget that **covert** involvement (think time) is a prerequisite to getting **overt** involvement (the answers to our questions). Phrasing questions with words like

Consider....

Imagine....

Take a few moments and consider....

Think about....

invites students to participate covertly. And—give them the time needed to think! (For more ideas, review page 80.)

If you're going to ask the question and provide think time before getting an answer, hold all students accountable for thinking or mentally constructing an answer. This is the tricky part. Remember level of concern in the Motivation chapter? Raising level of concern is the best insurance we have that we're getting both covert and overt behavior. To raise that feeling of *accountability* for thinking, students need to know that you're not using that old traditional technique of calling on volunteers for answers. Let them know that when you phrase your question:

I'll be calling on a non-volunteer....

Be ready in case I call on you....

You'll all have to prepare an answer....

If students don't sense accountability for participation, they're back to the *Law of Least Effort.*

On the other hand, be careful that level of concern isn't too high, turning into anxiety and interfering with responding. Not giving enough time to think of the answer may be so frustrating you get an "I dunno" for a response. Or for some students just having to answer in front of the whole class can provoke anxiety. Find other strategies to get them involved besides just question-answer. Using cooperative learning ("Go around your table and each person share your answer.") and partner work ("See if your partner agrees with your answer.") can build in think time as well as appropriate level of concern.

Check Yourself Out!

Below are two sets of questions. Which set is most effective for eliciting active participation during discussion and why? What's wrong with the other set?

Set I: Questions about Goldilocks
1. Look at me when you are ready to whisper the name of the middle size bear. (Time) Whisper the name.

2. All of you imagine the possible reasons for leaving the house unlocked and going out for a stroll. (Time)
Share your answers in your team.

3. You need to pick a side for the following debate: should Goldilocks be arrested for breaking and entering? (Time)
Jot down on your think pad what your reasoning will be.
(MBWA—teacher monitors by walking around)
Now debate this at your table.

<u>Set II: Questions about Cinderella</u>
1. Who did Cinderella dance with at the ball?
(A student blurts out "the prince.")

2. The prince tried the glass slipper on the stepmother before trying it on Cinderella. Joe, what would have happened in the story if the shoe had fit the stepmother?

3. Do you think there is a moral to this story? Sandy? (Sandy had the first hand up.)

Did you say "Obviously, the first set is the best!" The questions gave students time to think, accountability was built in (note the underlined words), and all students were overtly involved. The second set lacked structure. That is, they allowed for blurting out (probably by a high achiever) and gave permission to others to follow the *Law of Least Effort*! Only one student was actively involved (overtly) at any given time.   How'd you do?

During Small Group and Independent Work
This becomes a scheduling issue. Do you provide as much opportunity for small group and independent work as you do direct instruction and whole group discussion? One secondary teacher has her daily routine organized into
- Entry task—work independently on journal entry (10 minutes)
- Direct instruction/whole group discussion (20 minutes)
- Small group activity (10 minutes)
- Independent practice (8 minutes)

While this routine occupies four days of the week, she reserves one day a week for learning centers and/or project work.

Motivating <u>All</u> to Be Involved

Scheduling in opportunities for active involvement by students doesn't guarantee they'll participate. Glasser (1990) suggests that less than 15% of our students do high-quality academic work in school. While they are capable of doing the work, they don't believe it's worth doing. If we're going to get active participation by all, we must examine the *quality* of task.

Quality Tasks

Haberman (1991) presents a convincing argument that good teaching is "more evident in what the students are doing than in the observable actions of the teacher." His definition of quality tasks and evidence of good teaching include:

- Students are engaged with issues they regard as vital concerns.
- Students are helped to see big ideas and not merely engaged in the pursuit of isolated facts.
- Students are involved in planning how they will be actively involved.
- Students are involved in a real-life experience.
- Students are given opportunity to self-evaluate, fine-tune and polish their work.

Variety of Overt Strategies

Use the theory of multiple intelligences (Gardner, 1983) as a tool to analyze the variety of opportunities you provide for active involvement. Opportunities for overt involvement should include:

1. Linguistic, oral and written: storytelling, poems, journals....

2. Musical: composing, rhythm instruments, listening, singing, performing....

3. Logical-mathematical: ordering objects, comparing, manipulating objects, pattern-making, problem making and solving....

4. Spatial: imagery, observations of the visual world, working with 2- and 3-dimensional forms, sculpting, the arts....

5. Bodily-kinesthetic: athletics, dance, acting, mime....

6. Personal
• Interpersonal: self-analysis & evaluation, recognizing one's feelings....
• Intrapersonal: recognizing feelings of others, social skills, cross-age tutoring, helping opportunities....

Opportunities to use the theory of multiple intelligences and provide for active participation can be found
- during learning centers
- when students are working on projects
- during cooperative learning activities
- during literature club
- during writers' workshop
- while writing in reflective journals

What else can you add to this list? (Details on how to organize these activities can be found in *Managing a Diverse Classroom,* Cummings.)

Don't Forget Congruency

"Cutesy" gimmicks to get students actively involved mean nothing if they're not related to the learning. A "thumbs up if you agree, down in you disagree" after every student response becomes more an exercise in thumb movement than thinking! And, don't imagine that just because your students are taking notes that they have their minds actively involved in the learning.

Just because students are painting a mural (stimulating spatial intelligence) doesn't mean they are developing a better understanding of a key social studies concept. "...the key to the effectiveness of an activity is its cognitive engagement potential—the degree to which it gets students thinking actively about and applying content...." (Brophy & Alleman, 1991). Brophy & Alleman add that many of the activities suggested for expanding the intelligences or increasing motivation and active participation are

- cumbersome or time-consuming—not offering enough cognitive engagement potential to justify their use
- are busy work
- are built around peripheral ideas, not major concepts
- are not at an appropriate level of difficulty; prior knowledge is not in place

Summary

If *all* children are to be given equal opportunity to learn, then *all* children need to be actively involved in the learning!

Children who are treated as if they are uneducable
almost invariably become uneducable.
Kenneth B. Clark

Chapter 9

Mental Set

Ready...Set...Go

Can you:
- **describe what a mental set does for the learner**
- **give examples of the components of a mental set: focus (motivation), retention (association & organization), and active involvement**

In a track meet the runner has to prepare well to get out of the blocks for a good start. The starter aids that trackster by giving a few simple commands that ensure all will be off to a good start. At the call of "ready" the runner focuses in on the starter. At the command of "set," the runner comes up into the starting position, mentally preparing for the starting pistol. All previous races and starts are transferred into this race. "Go"...the runner springs forward into yet a new race, the outcome at the finish line.

Those starting commands are not unlike what the teacher does to *mentally* prepare students to learn. The teacher, too, wants to focus the students at the initial stages of learning. You have to gain entrance to working memory before filling it with information! You want to give students a chance to see what they already know about this lesson, to associate past learning with the present. You want all learners off to a "good start" immediately, not eventually have them tune in.

Let us show you how powerful this experience can be. Fill in the blanks in the following paragraph. The first letter or letters are provided for you.

Anyone interested in te_____ is concerned about c_____. It's hard to imagine te_____ sch_____ without them. Although they can sometimes be bothersome, we t_____ them. When things go wrong, we sometimes blame the p_____, instead of accepting responsibility for the consequences ourselves.

Check your answers:
Anyone interested in **television** is concerned about **commercials**. It's hard to imagine **television schedules** without them. Although they can sometimes be bothersome, we **tolerate** them. When things go wrong, we sometimes blame the **product,** instead of accepting responsibility for the consequences ourselves.

How did you do? Now, we know this may have been a negative experience for you, but try to learn from it.

Students come to us with a tremendous backlog of information and experience. It is important to capitalize on that backlog of information and bring it to the new learning. A teacher has to be sure to capitalize on the "right" backlog of information and bring it forward.

Set gets students ready to learn. Here's an example. A teacher was about to begin a unit on anthropology. She started the class by dumping the waste basket all over the floor. Then she had students come up and begin to sort through the contents to find out something about the classes that had been there that day. They found that there had been a social studies class, an English class, and that some students had had a snack of oranges, milk, and assorted junk food. In addition, someone was meeting Mike at the game Friday!

The teacher then went on to say: "That's just like what archeologists do. They sort through the things left behind from other civilizations to find out about who lived there and how they lived. That's what our new unit is all about. In fact, you'll be able to describe archeologists and their contributions to our understanding of past human life."

READY: Drawing the relationship between leftovers from the wastebasket and those of ancient civilizations. Students were told what they would have to do with this information.

GO: Overtly, some students were sifting through remains; covertly, others were watching.

In planning a set, decide:

READY: How can I motivate (focus) the learner? Something novel or different might capture their interest.

SET: How can I provide meaning for the lesson by association and organization. Eliminate having the student wondering "What's this all about?" Point out logical relationships between any old learning and the new. Let the student know the organization for this new lesson.

GO: How can I actively involve all the learners (either overtly or covertly) so I can speed up their learning?

Here's another example of set. Try to identify the principles of motivation, meaning, and active involvement.

A class was working on reducing fractions. The teacher began a lesson with, "Suppose you came home and your mom had baked an apple pie that really looked good to you. You really wanted some. She said you could have 25/100s of that pie. Raise your hand if you know how much you could have." No hands went up. The teacher continued: "Well, let's suppose that mom said you could have 1/4 of the pie, then would you know?" They did! "That's what we'll work on today, reducing complicated fractions to simpler ones. You'll be able to take any of these fractions listed on the board here and give me a simpler form."

How did this teacher do?

READY: It is more interesting when the students see themselves in the situation—in this case, eating apple pie!

SET: There is an association made between a fraction they already know (1/4) and what they will learn (equivalent "complicated" fractions).

GO: All students had a chance to think about how much pie they'd get. They raised their hands to indicate which fraction they knew, which one they didn't.

The next example of a mental set took much less time but was equally as powerful. The teacher simply said, "Who would like to NEVER miss a subtraction problem again?" All hands went up! "Great, we'll learn one little trick that will keep you from missing any more subtraction problems!"

READY: Interest was captured with the thought of not missing any more problems.

SET: The teacher knew all of the students had missed problems in the past and could relate to the experience.

GO: Active involvement was instantaneous when all hands eagerly went up in the air.

Let's look at these three attributes of mental set in more detail.

READY: Think about what your students are like at the beginning of most lessons. Their minds could be almost anywhere—on what had happened just previous to the new lesson—gazing out the window—thinking about lunch time—thinking about home. You don't want them to "tune in" to the lesson in the middle; you need them to be with you from the start. This is a perfect place to use a motivational technique, to create immediate focus. Gain access to their working memory. This can be done with "self" (anything related to them personally is more interesting), a discrepant event (something they're not expecting, something novel), feeling tone (get them emotionally involved; your own enthusiasm for the new lesson may be just the thing!), humor or drama, or raising level of concern by communicating to them what is expected in the lesson, what their goal should be. Students tend to live up to expectations. We have ample evidence indicating that retention of verbatim information is increased by simply providing prequestions and objectives at the beginning of a lesson.

SET: Essentially, learning is linking new information to prior information. It'll be difficult for students to activate prior learning if the new lesson is disorganized or unclear. Therefore, maximize the learning of the new material by:
1. providing an overview of the lesson
2. outlining the information
2. listing the objectives

If students are about to _read_ a new chapter, have them preview the chapter, looking at section headings, bold print and italics, objectives, chapter questions, and graphics. Hold them accountable for previewing the chapter by having them
1. predict what they will learn from the chapter
2. outline the chapter, using the chapter headings
3. graphically show what the chapter includes

In addition, help the students actually make the links with the following activities:

- Brainstorm everything you already know about _____ _____.
- What experiences have you had that are similar to the one we're about to study? Discuss them in your team.
- Make a chart showing what you know and what you'd like to know about this topic.
- Look at the vocabulary list that we'll have for this lesson. Put a "+" by words you know; a "?" if you can't define it.
- Predict what you think this topic will include. On what prior knowledge do you base your prediction?

GO: Get students involved! Using the activities described above builds in that involvement. Don't settle for one or two students answering the "set" questions; get *all* minds involved. Have students work on the questions/activities in small groups. Or use the activity as a "warm-up" (an independent activity when students enter class).

Mental set is not reserved for the beginning of lessons only. Remember task analysis? You may need to provide set at the beginning of a new step in the task analysis. For example, in teaching a lesson on reading Roman numerals, the teacher just completed the step that when the smaller numeral is to the right of a larger one, you *add* (XI equals 10 + 1). The set for the next step was:

"Now the next step is just the opposite (pointing to the differences). When the smaller numeral is to the left, you do what?" The students said "subtract."

Set should not take so long that students lose time that could be spent in the new learning. Set shouldn't be so exciting that students can't focus on the lesson objective. Rather, the creative teacher will add just the right amount of motivation, meaning, and active involvement to get students _ready to learn_!

Summary

A mental set gets students ready to begin a lesson. First, it captures their attention. Then, it establishes in the learners' minds what they're going to learn and at the same time hooks the lesson into prior learning. It invites the learner to be an active participant in the lesson. Minds aren't always ready for learning—they must be prepared.

The growth of the human mind is still high adventure, in many ways the highest adventure on earth.
Norman Cousins

Chapter 10

Planning Better Lessons

Can you:
- **compare long-range to weekly and daily lesson planning**
- **describe the lesson designs: 3-Prong; 6-Step; Social Skill**
- **label an objective as: information, concept, process/skill, social, or thinking skill**
- **describe planning strategies applicable to each type of objective**

We want our students to learn *because* of us not in *spite* of us! We need to plan certain events into our lessons that increase the odds that our students will learn. These events are based upon research on how human beings learn. When we build them into our lessons, we have systematically promoted learning.

Where to Begin?

There are so many decisions to make in this planning process! The "big" decisions that involve scope and sequence of the curriculum have usually been done for you at the district level. Then where do you actually begin your planning? We'd suggest beginning with long range estimates of units you hope to teach each month. This long range plan helps you estimate content coverage for the year—if everything goes the way you want it to (does it ever?)!

Unit Plan

Think big...start small. Begin with a theme in mind. If possible, integrate it across the curriculum. Remember congruency—don't force a fit.

Theme: **Topic:**

	Reading	Lang. Arts	Science	Social Studies	Math
Sept.					
October					

Teachers in multi-age settings might have a unit plan like this:

Theme: **Topic:**

	Reading Lab	Writing workshop	Learning Centers	Class Meeting	Projects/ Menus
Sept.					
October					

Or, you may plan your unit around a block (i.e., Communication Arts) or for a single subject (i.e., Social Studies). Even if this is the case, you can consider building in social skills and thinking skills to support your basic content objectives. On the following pages are examples of unit plans designed this way.

Theme: Relationships

Topic: Fairy Tales

READING	WRITING	THINKING SKILLS	COOP. STRATEGY	SOCIAL SKILL
Red Riding Hood The Three Bears The Three Pigs	Keep a journal: • characters you like • how you feel as you read	comparing Venn diagram	think-pair-share round-table	encouraging others taking turns
TLWBAT • retell story	TLWBAT • compare 2 tales in Venn diagram	predicting	chips	asking questions
• describe characters	• prepare a character trait grid	sequencing	interviewing	
• predict ending	• write a new ending	defining problems		
• order sequence of events	• write a story structure for your favorite fairy tale			
• identify character traits				
CONCEPTS character sequence trait solution problem				

167

Theme: Solving Conflict

Topic: World War II

INFORMATION OBJ.	CONCEPTS	COMBINED	THINKING SKILLS
TLWBAT explain the growth of dictator nations leading to war	dictator communism	TLW identify the relationships/patterns leading up to WWI & WWII.	identify relationships & patterns problem solving
TLWBAT describe the rise of the Nazi state	war	Compare the terms ending actual fighting in WWI & WWII.	comparing
TLWBAT describe American neutrality while Germ. conquered Europe	cold war	Compare key concepts and issues involved in 4 major wars.	webbing/mind mapping ordering Venn diagram
TLWBAT explain how the attack on Pearl Harbor brought the US into the War		Evaluate the impact of WW II on America to-day.	
			SOCIAL SKILLS
TLWBAT describe major events during War			how to disagree in an appropriate way
TLWBAT describe the UN plan for world peace			anger management
TLW describe friction between US & Russia			empathy-recognize feelings

168

Weekly Planning

This is generally abbreviated lesson planning. That is, such decisions as practice activities (*warm-ups*), the objective, practice on a new objective, and materials are included. What we jot down is more a reminder to us of what we want to do, what materials we'll need, rather than a complete lesson plan. Some hints for filling out your plan book include:

• Abbreviate when possible.

TLW	The learner will
TLWBAT	The learner will be able to
WU	warm-up
Obj	objective
Set	mental set
Inp	input
Mod	model
GP	guided practice
IP	independent practice
PR	student processing
Mat	materials
LC	learning centers

• Place an "*" by any objective that has a fully developed lesson plan in the teacher manual. This is a useful reminder for both you and your substitute. You might even code your textbooks (i.e., *World Civilization* = WC).

• Color code when possible. For example, write your warm-up activities in red pencil to indicate distributed practice on a previously taught objective. Color code when "specialists" are teaching. Use either erasable pen or pencil to allow for changes as the week progresses. Or, format your computer and make adjustments as you go.

WEEKLY PLANS

WEEK OF   **Theme:** Problem Solving

1		
MONDAY	**SUBJECT** Heading **TIME**	**SUBJECT** Writing **TIME**
	WU: what does a detective use to solve a case? Inp - vocabulary words Mat - Encyclopedia Brown IP - Read 1/2 Coop - predict ending IP - Read last half GP - Numbered heads: story comprehesion questions	Obj: TLW write an original mystery. Inp - intro template: crime, suspects, clues, motive IP - Prewrite
TUESDAY	Literature clubs Each group reading a different mystery IP - USSR Coop - clubs meet to discuss chapter	Writers' Workshop Continue through each stage of writing process Conference individual students

SUBJECT Math   **TIME**
Obj: TLW use steps in solving word/story problems Inp - Venn diagram-how detective work is like word problems in math M - think aloud GP - work w/partner, solve problem using steps
Obj: TLW find real life math. problems in newspaper Set - what's your favorite section of paper to read Inp/Mod - show how to recognize real-life math. problem in one section IP - corners of room, each with different section;

170

Lesson Designs

There is no one best format for writing a lesson. Three formats will be shared here. You will find that one format works best for one type of objective while another may best fit the needs of a different type of objective. The formats are:

3-Prong
for all types of objectives (concepts, procedures, information, etc.); for projects, self-directed lessons

6-Step
for classroom management objectives, review lessons, shorter lessons

Social Skill
for social skill objectives

3-Prong Model

You've really been introduced to an abbreviated form of this model earlier in this book. We've just added more detail to it here. This model is most appropriate when you have a lesson that has several steps in the task analysis. When these steps are incremental and you want to check to be sure one step is mastered before going on to the next, this model encourages you to think:

1. What is the step or main idea?
2. How will this step be presented?
3. How should students process the information (construct meaning)?

These decisions translate into the "3-prongs":

1	2	3
Task Analysis	Input Model	Student Processing

Another way of describing this model is comparing it to textbook writing. Let's make your lesson analogous to the textbook and your objective analogous to the title of the text. Because there is so much information in the text, it is organized into chapters. Readers tackle one chapter at a time...just as learners should tackle only one step at a time in a task analysis. Each chapter is filled not only with text that provides many examples but also graphics for the visually inclined. We plan our examples and models for our lessons, too (input/model). Note that this does not mean the lesson is teacher centered. That is, the teacher makes the decision for *how* the information is to be delivered. Perhaps a movie, guest speaker, or a hands-on experiment will be more effective for getting ideas across than direct teacher explanation and models. (A model of an indirect lesson can be found at the end of the next chapter.)

Typically at the end of each chapter there are questions testing mastery of the information in that chapter. When our learners have "filled their short-term memory" or finished one step in the lesson's task analysis, we need to have them process the information before adding more. As students process the information, the teacher is monitoring their answers, measuring the degree of mastery of that step. This provides a necessary checking point so that we don't "...continue to lecture on navigation while the ship is going down!" (James H. Boren)

When our lessons involve skill development, independent practice is provided at the end where learners put all of the steps together. Or, if the lesson requires mastery of a body of information, a closure activity requiring students to organize all of the information might be added.

Subject:		Date:	
Objective(s)			**Materials**
PROCESS/SKILL INFO CONCEPT SOCIAL/AFFECT THINKING SKILL			
Set			
HOOK TO FUTURE HOOK TO PAST ADV. ORGANIZER INTEREST			
Diagnosis			

	TASK ANALYSIS	INPUT/MODEL	STUDENT PROCESS
1.			
2.			
3.			
4.			
5.			

Independent Practice or Closure	
	3-PRONG

By Carol Cummings, Ph.D. using "Plan To Teach" © 1990 Teaching, Inc.

Subject: Reading		Date:

Objective(s) TLWDU of the story elements of problem/solution in book: "Stone Soup"; TLW develop fluency in reading "Stone Soup"

(PROCESS/SKILL) INFO (CONCEPT) SOCIAL/AFFECT THINKING SKILL

Set Your problem is that you must plan a meal with only the food or ingredient I give you.

HOOK TO FUTURE   HOOK TO PAST   ADV. ORGANIZER (INTEREST)

Diagnosis na

Materials
kettle
mixing stick
vocabulary cards
chart paper
tape of story
copies of Stone Soup

	TASK ANALYSIS	INPUT/MODEL	STUDENT PROCESS
1.	TLWBAT read new vocabulary words.	Pass out 1 vocabulary word per table; ask group to plan a meal using this word. Words: carrots, turnips, bone, water, potatoes	Small group discussion: how to use their food to make a meal
2.	TLW generate potential solutions to problem. (Story structure: problem-solution)	List student generated solutions on chart paper.	Students brainstorm solutions in small group first.
3.	TLWD understanding of story.	Play audio tape of story. Ask comprehension questions at specific intervals. Call on individuals—after they check with partner.	Follow text of story while listening to tape Partner/then individual responses
4.	TLW predict outcome of story.	Stop story in middle—List student predictions on chart paper—after small group discussion; discuss solution at end of tape	Students make predictions as to how problem will be solved in small groups first
5.	TLW orally read story to study buddy.	Monitor partners reading	With study buddy, take turns reading story to each other—alternating paragraphs

Independent   Practice or Closure

TLW use new vocabulary words in a story. (Integrating reading/writing)

TLW experience sharing by bringing one ingredient for soup to be made in class.

3-PRONG

By Carol Cummings, Ph.D. using "Plan To Teach" © 1990 Teaching, Inc.

Subject: Social skills/problem solving		Date:

Objective(s) TLWD skill in problem solving.

PROCESS/SKILL   INFO   CONCEPT   [SOCIAL/AFFECT] [THINKING SKILL]

Materials

Situation cards
My problem template
Temper tantrum cards

Set What's a problem? We're going to become the best problem
solvers. Our goal: to think about different ways to solve prob.
[HOOK TO FUTURE] [HOOK TO PAST] ADV. ORGANIZER   INTEREST

Diagnosis

TASK ANALYSIS	INPUT/MODEL	STUDENT PROCESS
1. TLW decide what the problem is.	Define: mystery; difficult to decide what to do; you might be upset; give ex: lost library book, forgot lunch	On your think pad, list problems you've had; share in group
2. TLW list all of possible solutions to problem (choices you have to solve problem)	Take 1 problem at time (ie lost book); list choices on board (use ex. of chart 'My problem'); Ex: forgot lunch- go without,tell tchr,go office	Given a new problem (i.e. you broke a window), what are your choices? List in your team (on 'My problem' template)
3. TLW explain the consequences/results of each choice	Go to consquences column on chart; list for each choice (i.e. starve, tchr loan you a ticket, office call home)	Take your problem choices you made in step 2 and describe in writing the consequences for each
4. TLW pick the best choice and do it	Model arranging the choices in order from best to worst. Give rationale for each.	Team rank orders choices on their own chart from best to worst; tell which one they'd pick & why
5. Decide if choice worked or if need to make another choice	Read problem: John forgot his homework....(What would happen if ....)	In teams, take one solution each, role play that solution and its consequence; tell if they liked that consequence

[Independent   Practice] or Closure

Situation cards: "What would happen if......." (use one card
per practice session; work in teams, each team then share
solution they'd pick with whole class)

Temper tantrum cards: same as above

3-PRONG

By Carol Cummings, Ph.D. using "Plan To Teach" © 1990 Teaching, Inc.

6-Step Lesson Design

This is probably the design most familiar to you.

1. **Objective**	share the objective
2. **Set**	get attention; review prerequisites
3. **Input**	present the new material
4. **Model**	provide visual support
5. **Guided Practice**	elicit student response while teacher provides immediate feedback
6. **Independent Practice**	students given opportunity to proceed at own pace to practice material (includes small group practice)

Rosenshine (1986) describes these steps as "teaching functions," using somewhat different labels:
1. Review
2. Presentation (includes stating the objective, input, and model)
3. Guided practice
4. Corrections and feedback
5. Independent practice
6. Weekly and monthly reviews

Rosenshine found this pattern of instruction most effective when teaching a well-structured skill.

We've found this pattern, when used for lesson planning, works best with small amounts of material or relatively short lessons. For example, a 15-minute primary lesson on how to make the letter "m" might be appropriate for this design. This design also lends itself to classroom management lessons (i.e., how to line up; keep an assignment sheet). A

176

55-minute lesson on photosynthesis, however, might best be planned using the 3-Prong model.

When a lesson is planned using the 6-Step, vertical sequence, it's not unusual for the teacher to teach "vertically"; that is, the bulk of the presentation precedes guided practice. Anything written in list form tends to be followed sequentially, one step before the next.

Even with the addition of teacher questions during the presentation (input/model), adequate processing time is often missing. Rowe's research (1983) demonstrated the effectiveness of 2-minute processing opportunities after 8-10 minutes of instruction at the high school. The 3-Prong lesson design allows for small chunks of information to be presented and student processing of that information before going on to the next chunk.

6-Step with practice. When your students need a review (Webster: to view or see again) of information previously taught, this is a great design. Let's first distinguish between review and practice. Review is to study the material again. Perhaps students had the same objective a year ago but need a "refresher". In this case, it takes very little time for the teacher to jog learners' minds about the material. The 6-Step, or "vertical teaching" is appropriate here, with the teacher reviewing the necessary information (input and modeling). If the goal of the lesson is practice, that is, the learners are to "do" the objective or perform the skill again to maintain proficiency, then the input and/or models are elicited from the students, to make sure their practice is "perfect practice"!

Subject:	Date:

Objective(s)

Set

Input

Model

Guided practice

Independent practice

Materials Needed

6-STEP

By Carol Cummings, Ph.D. using "Plan To Teach" © 1990 Teaching, Inc.

Subject: Classroom management　　　　　　　**Date:** Sept 6

Objective(s)

TLW work on a warm-up assignment when entering class each day.

Set

How many of you have ever had a job? Were you expected to show up to work on time? Would you be paid if you didn't? Were you expected to begin socializing or begin your work? Why? Compare to 'job' of being a student. Responsibility: to learn. Pay off: grades. Upon entering, chance for distributed practice; explain 1,1,1,4 practice schedule you'll use. Explain how many points toward grade students will earn for warm-up.

Input

1. Be in class by bell.
2. Take seat and begin working on assignment on overhead at front of room. Write it in your journal. Warm-ups will change daily: daily oral language (M); d.o. analogy (T); d.o. geography (W); d.o. math (Th) freewrite in journal (F)
3. If you finish early, select any other quiet activity.
4. You earn 5 points a day. Teacher will check warm-ups every few weeks by looking at your journal.
5. All tests will include questions from warm-ups. Answers to warm-ups will be given immediately after doing them, correct your own. They will be a good review before a test.

Model

Role play what is meant by words 'in class on time'. Show students coming through door vs. in classroom on way to desk.

Guided practice

Have warm-up ready for that day. Have class step outside door, come in again as if it were the beginning of the class period. Go through entire warm-up activity, including correcting them.

Independent practice

Be sure to include a warm-up on board every day. Check journals in 2 or 3 days. Emphasize points earned.

Materials Needed

warm-up on board

6-STEP

By Carol Cummings, Ph.D. using "Plan To Teach" © 1990 Teaching, Inc.

Social Skill Lesson Plan

Now this plan ought to look familiar...it's similar to the 6-Step plan introduced earlier. Because social skills do not involve the teaching of new, complex or difficult content, this vertical format for planning and teaching is appropriate. Note the differences in this plan with the 6-Step: group practice (rather than guided), evaluate/process (accomplished immediately after group practice), and transfer of training (rather than independent practice).

Group practice. "Social" implies skills designed to promote "pleasant companionship with one's friends or associates" (thanks, again, Webster!). Consequently, this step needs to allow for small group interaction so that skill can indeed be practiced. It is still "guided practice" in that the teacher is monitoring the groups and/or a student recorder is appointed in each team to record the group's attempts at practicing the social skill.

Evaluate or process. During the guided practice step in the 6-Step design, the teacher provides feedback to students regarding the accuracy of their responses. In social skill practice, this might be done with individual groups while the teacher is monitoring. However, time is also taken at the end of the small group practice session to analyze successful use of the social skill. Students may do this privately with a self-appraisal instrument. For example:

Listening skills	Yes	No
I look at the speaker. I encourage the speaker to talk. I let the speaker finish. I question the speaker. I smile and nod to show interest. I ignore distractions about me. I can improve by_____		

Or, the recorder in each team could provide feedback and the team evaluate their use of the skill. The teacher might give the results of the data collected while monitoring ("clipboard cruising") to the whole group and/ or might ask for whole group comments on skill usage.

Transfer of training. Yes, this is the equivalent of "independent practice" in the 6-Step model. The emphasis here, however, is on *transfer*. To maximize transfer of the social skill to other situations, homework assignments are recommended (Goldstein et al., 1980). These assignments require students to use the social skill taught in another situation and to record how successful they were. For example, a homework log to encourage social skill practice might include:

Social Skill:

Steps in process:

I tried this skill with:

What I did (said) was:

This is what happened:

I felt:

Subject:	Date:

Objective(s)

Set

Input

Model/Role play

Group practice   **Monitoring:**   TEACHER   STUDENT RECORDER

Evaluate/process: INDIVIDUAL   COOP GROUP   TEACHER   WHOLE GROUP

Transfer of training

Materials Needed

SOCIAL SKILL

By Carol Cummings, Ph.D. using "Plan To Teach" © 1990 Teaching, Inc.

Subject: Social Skills   **Date: Feb. 20**

Objective(s)

The learner will deal with anger effectively.

Set

Think of times you've been angry. What happened? Describe what typically happens when you're angry. (Set up a role play with another student, demonstrating an effective and ineffective way of dealing with anger.) Today's goal: to deal with our anger more effectively. Motto: It's OK to be angry. It's how you handle your anger that counts.

Input

1. First you must identify the feeling anger and what caused it.
   Discuss: what do look like on the outside? How do you feel on the inside?
   Make a T-chart for anger (what it looks like; feels like)
2. When you have that feeling, stop and count to ten.
3. Consider your choices: tell the person you're angry, walk away, do a relaxation exercise.
4. Pick the best choice(s).

Model/Role play

Role play keeping a calm voice while telling someone you're angry. Role play walking away. Model relaxation exercise of taking a deep breath on count of 3; letting it out to count of 6 (continue for count of 4 and 5)

Group practice   **Monitoring:**   [TEACHER] STUDENT RECORDER

In teams, agree upon 3 situations that make teammates angry; list warning signs of the anger (teeth clenched, jaws tighten, hands sweat, etc.); take turns in group role playing which option you'd select in dealing with the anger. With a partner, one person practice the breathing exercise while the other does the counting

Evaluate/process: INDIVIDUAL   COOP GROUP [TEACHER] WHOLE GROUP

Share feedback collected while 'clipboard cruising'.

Transfer of training

1. Keep a journal for the week of events that made you angry; describe the choice(s) you
   made for dealing with that anger. Evaluate your choice.
2. Warm-ups each day will include sentence starters about anger: I show my anger by....
   The worst thing about getting angry is.....It feels good to control my anger because....
3. Current events bulletin board: encourage students to bring daily newspaper articles
   related to anger management (i.e., sporting events; world news)

Materials Needed

SOCIAL SKILL

By Carol Cummings, Ph.D. using "Plan To Teach" © 1990 Teaching, Inc.

Planning the Lesson—More Specifics

So far, we've given you 3 formats for planning lessons. Which one will you use? We'd like to provide some suggestions. If you are planning a lesson "from scratch" (it's not detailed for you in a manual), where do you start?

Did you say "with my objective, of course?" Great! Now you need to determine the intent of your objective. That is, are you trying to teach:

    information
    a process or skill
    a concept
    a social skill (or attitude, value or feeling)
    a thinking skill or strategy

This is not an exhaustive list of types of objectives; rather, these are the types taught in most classrooms. For example, social skills are just one type of affective objective. The affective domain includes objectives dealing with attitudes, values and feelings. (See Cummings, *Managing to Teach*, for more information on lesson planning in the affective domain; or, Cummings, *The Get-Alongs,* a curriculum guide for teaching social skills.)

VARIETIES OF LEARNING
(included in this chapter)

Cognitive	Affective
Information Process/Skill Thinking Skill Concept	Social Skill

---

Types of Objectives

Let's define each type of objective.

Information. Information objectives usually include several topics within a lesson where the intent is to learn a body of knowledge or content. For example:

TLW describe the main types of wrenches and their uses.

TLW explain the levels of Bloom's Taxonomy.

TLW list and explain the events leading up to the French Revolution.

Process. When the intent of the objective is to learn a skill or procedure or method of operation, it is a process. For example:

Given 10 objects up to 12 inches in length, TLWBAT measure them to the nearest eighth of an inch.

Given a computer disk, TLWBAT load it into an Apple computer.

Given a letter inquiring about the shipping of an order, TLW generate a letter in reply.

Concept. If learners are expected to establish a mental category into which they will classify things, ideas and people based upon specific criteria, you're teaching a concept. For example:

Given examples of 5 trees, TLWBAT categorize them into evergreen and deciduous.

Given descriptions of economic systems, TLWBAT label them as capitalism, socialism, or communism.

Given descriptions of 10 animals, TLWBAT classify them as vertebrate or invertebrate.

Social skill. If you are teaching students techniques to form cooperative and interdependent relationships with peers, you're teaching them social skills. For example:

Given a task to complete in a group, TLW demonstrate good listening skills.

Given an opportunity to work in a group setting, TLW encourage others to participate.

Thinking skill. Thinking skill objectives are not really a distinct category, apart from concepts or processes. That is, a thinking skill might be taught as a concept or a process, or perhaps even information!

TLWBAT explain the steps in the problem solving strategy (a process objective).

TLWBAT recognize bias in a selected reading.

(Once the *concept* "bias" has been taught, then the *process* of detecting bias in a reading selection is taught.)

TLWBAT describe how to preview a chapter. (information)

Why did we list thinking skills as a separate category if this type of objective can be described as either concepts, information or processes? Because we need to consciously identify and teach such skills along with traditional content. More importantly, when we have objectives at the higher levels of Bloom's Taxonomy, learners first need a lesson on how to execute this higher level task: the thinking strategy.

Combining thinking skill with other content. If you want your students to develop a proposal for energy conservation, you really have two objectives.

TLW use the problem solving process to develop a written proposal, *and*

TLWBAT describe the factors contributing to the energy shortage and the consequences of such a shortage.

Pretty big undertaking! (Review Chapter 3 for more examples of this type of objective.) You may find that you are planning two review lessons: one for the steps in problem solving, one for factors related to energy conservation. Because these review lessons will be relatively brief, the 6-Step plan for each might be most appropriate.

Hints for Teaching Each Type of Objective

You've made three major decisions so far: what is my objective; what type of objective is it (i.e., concept, social skill); and which lesson plan format shall I use. Now, it's time to plan the actual lesson. Chapter 11 is devoted to planning a lesson for concepts. We'll add more information now for other types of objectives.

Information. There are so many facts to be learned! And these facts connect to larger bodies of information. How do you ever get this information across? *Chunk it!* That is, organize the information into *meaningful* chunks. For example, we organize facts in history around periods. We might study a particular war in the chunks *before*, *during*, and *after*. We study seasonal change by organizing the information into *spring, summer, fall,* and *winter*.

Once the information is chunked, we let our students know how we've organized the lesson in our set:

"Today we'll examine the Civil War first in terms of the conditions leading up to it; then major events during the war; and finally, the aftermath of the war."

Or, provide a visual for students at the beginning of the lesson so they will see the divisions and recognize where you are in the lesson:

We'll divide today's lecture on the political spectrum into 4 parts:

Radical	Liberal
Conservative	Reactionary

Once the material has been divided up, you've announced the divisions to your students, what next?

- Let your students know when you've finished one point by summarizing it or simply stating that you're through with it.
- Give your students time to summarize one point cognitively before moving on to the next.
- Clearly state that you're beginning the next point.

What lesson plan formats lend themselves to this type of lesson? The 3-Prong works best with large bodies of information. But remember, even though you've organized the material, it doesn't mean that you *personally* have to present each point. Let's say you've selected an excellent film that covers all three of your points on the Civil War. What's preventing you from stopping the film after each major point has been made and letting the students process that information before turning it back on?

(Chunk #1)"Take a few minutes now and outline with the person sitting next to you the major events leading up to the Civil War."

(Chunk #2) "If you were given the responsibility of recording in a history journal the most important highlights of the Civil War, what would they be? Jot them down on a piece of scratch paper and be ready to share."

(Chunk #3) "In your teams, discuss the most significant outcomes of the war. What impact have they had on history today? Be sure to have one person in your team record your discussion."

Notice that for processing each point in the lesson or in designing an independent assignment at the end of the lesson, the activity must require some type of rehearsal or elaboration by the learner. Having students construct their own summary, develop their own outline, or generate relationships between ideas will create both better retention and comprehension of the information.

Process or skill. When we teach students how to construct a sentence or a paragraph, how to do long division, or how to deliver a persuasive speech we are teaching a process or skill. Task analysis is the place to begin with this type of objective. What are the small incremental steps the process can be broken into? "First you...then you...then you...and finally you...." Walk through the task yourself and verbally label the steps you are going through.

Once you've identified the steps, how many steps should you teach students at a time? If you decide on only one or two steps at a time, and there are many steps in the analysis, the 3-Prong model will best fit your planning needs. It structures the lesson into

Step #1 ➡ tell/show ➡ DO
Step #2 ➡ tell/show ➡ DO

For example, in teaching how to write a friendly letter, you decide that your first step is to teach the return address and date. You explain what needs to be included, you model it for the students, then you have them write it. Your next step is the greeting. Again, you explain what a greeting is, you give examples, then ask students to write one. Notice that the student processing of the skill is "doing it"—a qualitatively different strategy from that used in the processing of information.

Now if you're teaching this same lesson to older students who had the same skill taught in the primary grades, you may prefer the 6-Step lesson format. You may have decided it's not necessary to teach and practice one small step at a time. Whichever format you choose, though, the independent practice is likely to be to put all the steps together into one: write the letter.

Concept. We can plan lessons for concepts using the 3-Prong and the 6-Step. How do you decide which to use? Identify how many critical attributes you have, how familiar your students are with the concept, and whether you want to teach the attributes one at a time or all together! Teaching the concept "square" to first-graders would probably require teaching one attribute at a time: "Let's first find shapes with 4 sides." Use the 3-Prong for this lesson. Yet, third-graders could probably handle all of the attributes at once...the 6-Step design.

After you've selected your format for planning a concept lesson, the next important consideration is your mental set. Use an advance organizer in your set. Let your students know the broader category to which this concept belongs ("We'll study another type of shape") as well as other relevant auxiliary concepts ("We've already studied circles and triangles, which are also special types of shapes.")

For this type of objective, pay particular attention to planning your examples. Write out specific examples...don't simply write in "give many examples"! Those examples need to be exaggerated, not ambiguous, and familiar to your learners.

When you plan to have your learners practice or process the concept, have them distinguish exemplars from non-exemplars of the concept before they generate their own examples. Be sure to read Chapter 11 for more about concept teaching.

Social Skill. When using this format, remember you are essentially in the affective domain. That is, you want learners to *value* this skill, to use it voluntarily when interacting with their peers. Begin your lesson with an opportunity for your learners to express why this skill is important to them. Get them involved at an emotional level.

Perhaps the most difficult part of the plan is the task analysis of the skill. What are the small behavioral steps one goes through in demonstrating this skill? As adults we perhaps take the skill for granted or use it intuitively. If you want help in this area, we recommend *Skillstreaming the Adolescent* (Goldstein et al.) This book has carefully task analyzed the major social skills taught in school.

In planning your role play or model for your lesson, remember it should be expertly done—this is not the time to call upon the class clown! When the students move into group practice they are actually role playing or practicing what they observed earlier.

Feedback (praise or approval as well as specifics) on how the skill is being practiced is so critical in prosocial development, that this is built into the lesson plan. And, again, unless we structure into our plan opportunities to use the skill in other settings, we're not likely to get transfer.

Summary

If great teaching is a composite of preactive and interactive and self-correcting decisions (Porter & Brophy, 1988), then this chapter has assisted with that first step: preactive decisions.

If you fail to plan...
You plan to fail!
author unknown

Chapter 11

Concept Development Strategy

Can you:
- give the rationale for teaching concepts
- task analyze a concept
- describe how to select examples of a concept
- describe how to measure concept learning

Perhaps the most difficult lesson of all to plan well is a concept lesson. Because of this, this chapter is devoted to fine-tuning the planning of concept lessons.

As learners make sense out of their world, they are often categorizing that which they encounter. They are applying *concepts*. That is, you walk through a buffet, noting as you go along: "The *salads* look really fresh so I think I'll pass on the *entree*." Or, you visit a friend's new home and make comments like "What a lovely *kitchen*."

We could argue that concept learning is more important than learning facts. It would take too much time to present all of the <u>specific</u> instances of salad or entree or kitchen. Instead, it's more economical to teach the category salad and provide a few examples. This concept, then, can generalize across a wide variety of examples. We can walk into a restaurant and discriminate any salad from an entree. Instead of memorizing all countries that have a democratic form of government, it's more efficient to have the concept democracy so we can apply the concept to any country we learn about. Concept teaching prevents *information overload* (also known as *academic indigestion*)!

To begin with, what is a concept? It is a set of distinctive characteristics. To be an example of a concept, a "thing" must possess those characteristics. We give this set of characteristics a label or a name. For example the name for any polygon having 3 sides is triangle. While the concept is actually that bundle of distinctive characteristics, not the label, we'll use labels as we describe specific strategies for concept teaching.

We teach concepts so that students can identify those distinct features when they encounter them in new situations. If a student has the concept of ball, he will be able to recognize one. Without knowing the distinctive features of a ball, one might mistake a cantaloupe for a ball! We teach the critical features of concepts so they can transfer across a wide variety of situations. Teach what a noun **is**, not that fish, chair, and car are nouns. Concepts aren't learned the same way facts are learned, one at a time. Instead, concept teaching requires specific teaching strategies.

The easiest way to examine concept teaching is by using the teacher decisions we've presented in previous chapters:

I. What is my objective? (*Now,* you're teaching a concept.)

II. How shall I teach to my objective? (What congruent activities are best for concepts?)

III. When and how shall I monitor? (What's the best way to measure conceptual learning?)

Selecting the Objective

Write a clearly defined objective. What do concept objectives look like?

- Given any poem, TLWBAT identify literal and figurative language.
- Given any polygon, TLW identify whether it is an example or non-example of a square.

Task analyze the objective. After determining that we're teaching a concept and not factual information, we do a task analysis of the concept. That is, what are the *distinctive characteristics* of this concept? (Distinctive characteristics are also called *critical attributes*.) You might begin with a dictionary definition if it's a common concept. If that definition contains vocabulary (other concepts) not readily understood by your learners, get the dictionary definition of those, too. For example, the dictionary definition of square is: A closed figure having four equal sides and four equal angles. Because the concept angle may be new to young students, get that definition, too. Angle: two lines coming together to make a point; a corner. If the dictionary does not contain an adequate definition of your concept, it's time to start rummaging through textbooks. Good luck!

Take that definition and break it into a list of attributes. For square, the list is:

closed figure
4 sides
sides are same size
4 corners
corners are same size

Concepts with concrete (perceivable) attributes are the easiest to analyze. For example, the attributes of chair are: a seat, typically with four legs and a back for one person. As objects are categorized, it's possible to see if the object has all three attributes. Not all concepts are that easy to analyze: honesty, democracy, freedom.

Some concepts will have more attributes than you would want to teach, particularly if you're working with younger students. For example, cell: microscopic mass of protoplasm; bounded externally by semipermeable membrane; usually including one or more nuclei and various non living products; capable, alone or interacting with other cells, of performing all the fundamental functions of life; forming the least structural unit of living matter capable of functioning independently. (Thanks, Webster!) The junior-high science teacher may want to teach all of the above attributes (including the variable attributes) but a fourth-grade science teacher may select only the critical (or constant) attributes.

When doing the task analysis it is often helpful to begin with the broader category to which the concept belongs, before listing the individual attributes. For example:

> median: a statistical concept related to central tendency
> noun: a word
> period: a punctuation mark
> capitalism: an economic system

Then, continue your task analysis with the critical attributes.

Don't Forget Bloom's Taxonomy!
Knowing the critical attributes of a concept is exactly that: the knowledge level. For example:

1. The learner will be able to define a compound sentence as two complete sentences connected by a conjunction and punctuated in between with a comma.

We want students to be at the comprehension level, at least.

2. The learner will demonstrate understanding of compound sentences by underlining them in a given passage.

Better yet, take your objective to the application level.

3. The learner will use (apply) compound sentences in written work.

Teach to the Objective

Remember, when you teach to your objective, the keyword is *congruent*: all aspects of the lesson are related to the objective. The goal is to use time wisely. In concept development, you can expedite the learning by knowing the critical attributes of the concept and carefully selecting examples and non-examples of the concept to illustrate those critical attributes.

These decisions are critical whether you choose to teach the concepts directly (expository method) or through discovery (i.e., concept attainment method). Taught directly, the teacher would present the critical attributes, provide many examples and non-examples, then ask students to categorize new examples. In concept attainment, students compare/contrast the examples and non-examples (given by the teacher), categorize them, then try to explain or label the attributes. The teacher (usually) gives them the label for that cluster of attributes.

We will not discuss the merits of expository vs. discovery at this point. Some authors argue that the exposition method may be more efficient in teaching most concepts while others argue that discovery is more motivating. Whichever method is used, <u>examples</u> are the key to success.

Examples...examples...examples

Select many, many examples! Select them carefully! To help you in selecting examples to illustrate a concept, use these reminders:

1. Eliminate the irrelevant information (or, at least hold it constant). Irrelevant information only clutters up the concept.

- In teaching the length of the hands on a clock, cover up the numbers.
- When teaching quotations and punctuation, draw a diagram (eliminating the words).

" _____,"

- When teaching plot or theme, keep the rest of the story short, minimizing distracting information.
- Films often have too much information in them to help a student learn a new concept. Ask specific questions to aid students in filtering out the irrelevant information while viewing the film.

2. Exaggerate the important information.

- In illustrations, draw the critical attributes darker or larger; use arrows to point them out.
- Underline in colored chalk the critical information or highlight the attributes in a different color.
- Select really obvious examples, without any ambiguity.

3. Use meaningful examples.

- Find examples that the learner has encountered previously.
- To teach the concept fruit, use an apple or banana rather than a kumquat or lingonberry.

• To teach simile, "The sun is as round as an orange," is more familiar than "She looked defeated, like pop's old fedora."

4. Teach one critical feature at a time.
Most concepts contain more than one critical feature or attribute. For example, the two attributes of compound words are: a new word made from two smaller words and the new word contains the meaning of both smaller words. Working with very young children, encountering this concept for the first time, we would teach one critical attribute, providing many examples and practice on *just* recognizing a word made up of two smaller ones. Then we would teach the second attribute, providing examples and practice on it. If, however, we were reviewing the concept with older students who perhaps have encountered it previously, we might decide to present both attributes together.

Monitor and Adjust
So far, you've taught the critical attributes of a concept and provided lots of carefully selected examples. How do you know your students have conceptualized...they truly have the concept and not just a mechanical definition? Monitor them using the following strategies:

1. Have students pick out examples of the concept from non-examples. Be careful, though. Pick your non-examples as carefully as you picked your examples, using the hints given earlier.
> • Here are three shapes, which one is a *square*?
> • Which of these sentences are *figurative*?
> • Underline the *prepositional phrases* in the sentences.

You are using examples that weren't provided during the lesson, so the learner isn't just recalling information; rather, the learner is having to look for the presence or absence of the critical attributes.

2. Have students translate the critical features of the concept into their own words.

- Tell me why that is a *polygon.*
- Why did you label that country a *democracy?*

3. Ask students to give their own examples of the concept.

This monitoring strategy should not be used until the student has succeeded with the discrimination practice (#1) and the translation (#2). Students may now be at a stage where they can recognize and give even more ambiguous examples of a concept and may start to generalize. They begin to recognize and give examples of the concept even when it has irrelevant features.

Ideally, we take our students to the application level with the concept: using the concept in new situations. Provide situations with no cues for the identification and use of the concept. After giving a writing assignment, note whether figurative language was used. See if students spontaneously recognize and correctly label instances of a concept without any prompting. If so, they're at an application level!

Use highly familiar examples in teaching concepts.

Anderson & Faust

Check Yourself Out!

To teach any concept, first you must

_____

_____

You need many examples to illustrate the critical attributes. How will you select your first examples?

_____

_____

How will you know your students have mastered the concept and not just memorized information?

_____

_____

Did you say that first you would identify the critical attributes of the concept, then carefully pick your examples? Did you eliminate irrelevant information in your examples as well as exaggerate the important features? Of course, you only selected examples familiar to the learner for your initial examples. And, if the concept was new and/or difficult, you taught just one critical attribute at a time. Your students let you know the concept is understood when they can classify examples as either exemplars or non-exemplars of the concept, describe the critical features of the concept in their own words, and generate their own examples.

Summary

Concepts are the building blocks of ideas, principles, and generalizations. Concepts help us organize the vast amount of information in the world. Concepts help us communicate with one another more efficiently. While many concepts are learned just by interacting with our environment, others are taught directly. This chapter examined strategies useful for teaching concepts. The model on the next page should serve as a useful reminder of these strategies.

Nothing in education is so astonishing as the amount of ignorance it accumulates in the form of inert facts.
Henry Adams

Subject: Teacher plan for teaching concepts		Date:	

Objective(s) TLWBAT use the concept "_____" in an appropriate situation.

Materials

PROCESS/SKILL INFO [CONCEPT] SOCIAL/AFFECT THINKING SKILL

Set

HOOK TO FUTURE   HOOK TO PAST   ADV. ORGANIZER   INTEREST

Diagnosis

TASK ANALYSIS	INPUT/MODEL	STUDENT PROCESS
1. TLW know the critical attributes	Explain attributes	Describe attributes to a partner—using your own words
2. TLW understand the concept	Present 1 attribute at a time (if new or complex); many examples—eliminate irrelevant info; exaggerate imp. info; meaningful ex.	
3.	Design activities or questions to cause—interpretation or discrimination; translation or explanation; have students make up own examples	With a partner, pick out examples from non-examples; infer or summarize why; find your own example of the concept
4. TLW apply/use the concept	Select new and varied situations in which to use the concept	Use the concept with no prompts
5.		

Independent   Practice or Closure

3-PRONG

By Carol Cummings, Ph.D. using "Plan To Teach" © 1990 Teaching, Inc.

Subject: Plan—students "discover" concept attributes		Date:

Objective(s) TLWBAT identify a square.

PROCESS/SKILL INFO [CONCEPT] SOCIAL/AFFECT THINKING SKILL

Materials

Set

HOOK TO FUTURE HOOK TO PAST ADV. ORGANIZER INTEREST

Diagnosis

TASK ANALYSIS	INPUT/MODEL	STUDENT PROCESS
1. TLW know a square has 4 sides	This is a square ☐ This is one ☐ This isn't one △ Is this one? ☐	Watch; listen Signal yes or no
2. TLW know sides of square are the same size	This is one ☐ This is one ☐ This is not one ▭ Is this one? ▭	Watch; listen Signal yes or no
3. TLW know a square has 4 corners	This is one ☐ This is not one △ Is this one? ◁	Watch; listen Signal yes or no
4. TLW know the corners of a square are the same size	This is one ☐ This is not one ▱ Is this one? ☐	Watch; listen Signal yes or no
5. TLWBAT list the critical attributes of a square	Display examples and non-examples selected by class; Ask class to decide what a shape must have to be called a square	Working with a partner, write on think pad what a square must have

Independent   Practice or Closure

3-PRONG

By Carol Cummings, Ph.D. using "Plan To Teach" © 1990 Teaching, Inc.

Teacher attitudes and expectations can act as self-fulfilling prophecies. The effective teacher feels in control of the situation.

Brophy & Evertson

SUMMARY

Take the following mini-exam, to see if we accomplished our task:

On a scale of 1 to 5, decide what you believe.

true				false
1	2	3	4	5

When it comes right down to it, a teacher really can't do much because most of a student's motivation and performance depends on his or her home environment.

true				false
1	2	3	4	5

If I try really hard I can get through to even the most difficult or unmotivated students.

These two test items are predictors of a teacher's success in the classroom (Dembo & Gibson, 1985). If you were on the false side for the first and the true for the second, you've got the right attitude for classroom teaching!

Teachers have hundreds of decisions to make every hour. These decisions will make a difference in the learning that goes on in the classroom. We know that

TEACHING MAKES A DIFFERENCE!

GLOSSARY
(may include page numbers for additional information)

ACTIVE PARTICIPATION
Active responding by a student. It may be thinking (covert) behavior or observable (overt) behavior. Active participation increases the rate and degree of learning. However, just any activity will not do...only congruent student responding increases learning. (149)

AFFECTIVE DOMAIN
Referring to learning involving interest, attitudes and values and the development of appreciation. Krathwohl has categorized objectives in this domain into: receiving, responding, valuing, organization, and characterization.

ANALYSIS
Breaking material into parts and comparing or contrasting those parts. Analysis is the fourth level of Bloom's taxonomy. It enables a student to detect relationships among parts and the way they are organized. (35)

APPLICATION
Using appropriate generalizations and skills to solve a problem encountered in a new situation. The third level of cognition in Bloom's taxonomy. Activities designed at the application level provide practice in the transfer of learning. (34)

ASSOCIATION
The process of hooking or relating new information to information already stored in long-term memory for the purpose of adding meaning and increasing retention. (100)

ATTRIBUTION THEORY
Theory that describes the causes people place on their success or failure. Varies on three dimensions: internal or external; changeable or not; controllable or not. Ability, effort, task difficulty, and luck are used to explain success or failure. Helps explain student motivation. (126)

BLOOM'S TAXONOMY
A classification of cognitive objectives into 6 levels: knowledge, understanding, application, analysis, synthesis, evaluation. Serves as a guide in writing objectives, diagnosing

student behaviors, and planning activities to extend student thinking. (32)

CONCEPT
A name for a class of objects or events. Example: square is the concept name for any object having 4 equal sides and 4 right angles. A student understands a concept when she/he can discriminate between examples and non examples of the concept. (197)

CONGRUENT BEHAVIORS
Any actions in a lesson that match or target the intended objective. To teach to the objective, the teacher selects questions, activities, directions, explanations, and responses to student efforts that are appropriate to (congruent with) the objective. (57)

COVERT BEHAVIOR
Student responses that are not observable. Thinking about the desired learning. This level of active participation takes less time than an overt response but it cannot be monitored by the teacher. Allowing time for covert behavior (thinking) can increase the quality of the overt response. (79)

CRITICAL ATTRIBUTE
The distinctive features that make something what it is. Used to define a concept: all positive examples of a concept share this feature. Can be used to distinguish positive from negative instances of a concept. (203)

DIAGNOSTIC SURVEY
A method(s) of determining where a student's learning left off and new learning begins. May be informal (asking oral questions) or formal (written pretest). Usually designed from the task analysis (the sequential learnings leading to the final objective) using questions from easy to more difficult. Used to determine correct level of difficulty. (22)

ELEMENTS OF EFFECTIVE INSTRUCTION
A classification system of teacher decision making developed by Madeline Hunter and Ernie Stachowski. When teachers make consistent and conscious decisions during instruction, they increase the probability of student learning. The following are the four categories:
1. Select objectives near the correct level of difficulty

2. Teach to objectives
3. Monitor and make adjustments
4. Use principles of learning

EVALUATION
The level of thinking at which a person makes a judgment based on sound criteria. There is no right or wrong answer. Evaluation is the sixth level of Bloom's taxonomy. It involves a combination of other levels of the taxonomy. (35)

EXTRINSIC MOTIVATION
A variable of motivation. Increasing focus by using reinforcers (rewards) not related to the learning itself. The child focuses on a task in order to receive a payoff. Examples: doing task to earn a grade, points, star, etc. (142)

GUIDED PRACTICE
During the lesson the student practices what has been taught with close teacher monitoring to catch any mistakes before students practice independently. It gives the students successful original learning, promotes retention, and allows the teacher to monitor.

INTEREST
Something vivid, different, or meaningful to the learner. One of the variables of motivation. (140)

INTRINSIC MOTIVATION
When the task is the reward itself, the learner is motivated to stay on task (i.e., a student reads a book because she/he loves to read.) The incentive value of the task provides motivation.

KNOWLEDGE
The student recalls or recognizes information. The lowest or first level of cognition in Bloom's taxonomy. The student needs information that she/he can recall or locate before using that information at higher levels of cognitive complexity. (34)

KNOWLEDGE OF RESULTS
Providing the student with feedback about the adequacy of her/his response. This feedback should come immediately after student responses and it should be specific in terms of what the student has done well and what she/he might do to change.

A variable of motivation. It helps students focus on the task when they know how well they are doing. (130)

LEVEL OF CONCERN
Fear of losing something you want or need (success, status) will cause level of concern. There is little or no motivation with a low level of concern. A student may be unable to focus on a task with too much concern. (135)

LONG-TERM MEMORY
The component of the memory system that stores information for unlimited amounts of time; often called permanent storage.

MEANING
Building meaning into a lesson will increase both motivation and retention. Types of meaningfulness that affect learning are: meaningful items (vs. nonsense items), patterned material (vs. unorganized material), logical meanings and understood relationships, and knowledge of use. (97)

MENTAL SET
A teacher strategy to provide a mental preparedness for the new learning. Combines motivation to focus the student, active participation to involve the student, and meaning to transfer forward previous learning and hook it to the new. (155)

MODELING
Teaching using visual-spatial activities. Will increase rate and degree of learning as well as retention. (94)

MONITOR AND ADJUST
A process whereby the teacher elicits overt behavior from the students, checks that behavior, interprets it, and decides on appropriate adjustments. Adjustments may be in terms of content, teacher presentation, or principles of learning. It is the third category of teacher decision making in the Effective Elements of Instruction. Allows the teacher to check on the learning of students and to change instruction appropriately (teaching diagnostically). (75)

MOTIVATION
Refers to the focus, attention, or persistence of student behavior. This persistence or effort is determined by the students expectations to be successful on the task and the

perceived value of the task.   One of the principles of learning. Elements of motivation theory that can be used to increase focus are: success, knowledge of results, interest, level of concern, feeling tone, and intrinsic/extrinsic motivators. (123)

OBJECTIVE

The goal toward which teaching is directed. A clear statement of the content, thought process, and behavior of the learner. It may also contain the conditions for testing and the performance level required. (44)

OVERT BEHAVIOR

Observable behavior. One level of active participation. Overt behavior is elicited from students so the teacher can monitor student progress. It increases the learning by keeping students actively involved. (151)

PRACTICE

A strategy to aid retention of information. (115)

PROACTIVE

A characteristic Brophy factored out of the research to describe effective teachers. Refers to behavior initiated by the teachers themselves - in contrast to reactive behavior that less effective teachers exhibit in situations when students do something that forces them to make some sort of immediate reactive response. Proactive teachers predict possible undesirable situations or behaviors before they occur and attempt to solve or prevent them from occurring.

PRINCIPLES OF LEARNING

Fundamental processes identified by psychologists that improve the efficiency of learning. In this book the following principles of learning were discussed: motivation, retention, active participation, and mental set (a combination). (89)

PROCESSING

Causing students to do more than just read or hear the material one more time. Having students actually demonstrate understanding or ability to apply information will promote retention. (105)

RETENTION

The act of remembering or retaining learning. One of the principles of learning. Variables affecting retention (discussed in this book) are: meaning, modeling & multiple modalities, processing, and practice. (91)

SHORT-TERM MEMORY
Part of the memory system, also known as working memory, where very limited amounts of information (5-7 bits) can be held for but a few seconds of time before being processed into long-term memory or lost. (98)

SUCCESS
Refers to the feeling of achievement when one accomplishes a task. A variable of motivation. Success is more probable if tasks are set at the appropriate level of difficulty. If students believe they will be successful on a task, they're more likely to exert effort. (125)

SYNTHESIS
Refers to the putting together of parts into a whole using creative and original thinking. The fifth level of Bloom's taxonomy. The student must draw upon elements from many sources and put them together into a pattern new to the learner or resulting in a new product. (35)

TASK ANALYSIS
An identification of the sublearnings necessary to accomplish a given objective. The process of task analysis involves breaking a learning down into enabling skills and knowledge, and sequencing the list. Can be used to diagnose for correct level of difficulty, as a guide in teaching to an objective, and for monitoring and adjusting. (15)

TEACH TO AN OBJECTIVE
The part of the teaching-learning process in which the teacher chooses behaviors that are relevant or congruent to the intended objective. These behaviors (questions, directions, activities, explanations, responses to learner efforts) lead to the accomplishment of the objective and increase time on task. (53)

UNDERSTANDING
Refers to the student's grasping the meaning of the intended learning. This is the second level of Bloom's taxonomy. Evidence of comprehension or understanding includes being able to translate the information into another form of communication, interpreting by summarizing, and extrapolating or predicting based on trends identified. (34)

References

Anderson, R. & Faust, G. (1973). *Educational Psychology.* New York: Harper & Row.

Bettencourt, E., Gillett, M., Gall, M. & Hull, R. (1983). Effects of teacher enthusiasm training on student on-task behavior and achievement. *American Educational Research Journal, 20,* 435-450.

Beyer, B. (1987). *Practical Strategies for the Teaching of Thinking.* Boston: Allyn & Bacon.

Bloom, B. (1956). *Taxonomy of Educational Objectives: Handbook I: Cognitive Domain.* New York: McKay.

Bloom, B. (1976). *Human Characteristics and School Learning.* New York: McGraw-Hill.

Bloom, B. (1984). The search for methods of group instruction as effective as one-to-one tutoring. *Educational Leadership, 41,* 4-17.

Bransford, J. & Johnson, M. (1972). Conceptual prerequisites for understanding: Some investigation of comprehension and recall. *Journal of Verbal Learning and Verbal Behavior, 11,* 717-726.

Bransford, J. & Vye, N. (1989). A perspective on cognitive research and its implications for instruction. In L. Resnick & L. Klopfer (Eds.), *Toward the Thinking Curriculum: Current Cognitive Research.* Alexandria, Va.: ASCD.

Brophy, J. (1987). Synthesis of research on strategies for motivating students to learn. *Educational Leadership, 45,* 40-48.

Brophy, J. (1992). Probing the subtleties of subject-matter teaching. *Educational Leadership, 49,* 7, 4-8.

Brophy, J. & Alleman, J. (1991). Activities as instructional tools: A framework for analysis and evaluation. *Educational Researcher, 20,* 4, 9-23.

Brophy, J. & Good, T. (1986). Teacher behavior and student achievement. In M.C. Wittrock (Ed.), *Handbook of Research on Teaching.* New York: Macmillan Publishing Co.

Buzan, T. (1984). *Make the Most of Your Mind.* New York: Simon & Schuster.

Cameron, J. & Pierce, W. (1994). Reinforcement, reward, and intrinsic motivation: A meta-analysis. *Review of Educational Research,* 64, 3, 363-423.

Clark, C. & Yinger, R. (1979). Teachers' thinking. In P. Peterson & H. Walberg (Eds.), *Research on Teaching.* Berkeley, Ca.: McCutchan Publishing Corporation.

Collins, M. (1978). Effects of enthusiasm training of preservice elementary teachers. *Research in Teacher Education,* 29, 53-57.

Cummings, C. (1996). *Managing to Teach, Second Edition.* Edmonds, Wa.: Teaching, Inc.

Cummings, C. (1995). *Managing a Diverse Classroom.* Edmonds, Wa.: Teaching, Inc.

Cummings, C. (1993). *The Get-Alongs.* Edmonds, Wa.: Teaching, Inc.

Denbo, M. & Gibson, S. (1985). Teachers' sense of efficacy: an important factor in school improvement. *The Elementary School Journal,* 86, 173-184.

Doyle, W. (1983). Academic work. *Review of Educational Research,* 53, 159-199.

Doyle, W. (1986). Classroom organization and management. In M. Wittrock (Ed.), *Handbook of Research on Teaching.* New York: Macmillan Publishing Co.

Evertson, C., Anderson, C., Anderson, L., & Brophy, J. (1980). Relationship between classroom behavior and student outcomes in junior high math and English classes. *American Elementary Research Journal,* 17, 43-60.

Gage, N. & Berliner, D. (1984). *Educational Psychology ,Third Edition.* Boston: Houghton Mifflin Co.

Gagne, E. D. (1985). *The Cognitive Psychology of School Learning.* Boston: Little, Brown & Company.

Gardner, H. (1983). *Frames of Mind.* New York: Basic Books.

Garmston, R. & Wellman, B. (1995). Adaptive schools in a quantum universe. *Educational Leadership,* 52, 7, 6-12.

Glasser, W. (1990). The quality school. *Kappan,* 71, 6, 425-435.

Goldstein, A., Sprafkin, R., Gershaw, N. & Klein, P. (1980). *Skillstreaming the Adolescent.* Champaign, Ill.: Research Press.

Good, T. (1970). Which pupils do teachers call on? *Elementary School Journal*, 70, 190-198.

Goodlad, J. (1984). *A Place Called School*. New York: McGraw-Hill Book Co.

Haberman, M. (1991). The pedagogy of poverty versus good teaching. *Kappan*, 73, 4, 290-294.

Mager, R. (1968). *Developing Attitude Toward Learning*. Belmont, Ca.: Fearon Publishers.

Morgan, M. (1984). Reward-induced decrements and increments in intrinsic motivation. *Review of Educational Research*, 54, 5-30.

National Commission on Excellence in Education, (1983). *A Nation at Risk*. Washington D.C.: U.S. Department of Education.

National Council of Teachers of Mathematics, (1991). *Professional Standards for Teaching Mathematics*. Reston, Virginia: N.C.T.M.

Porter, A, & Brophy, J. (1988). Synthesis of research on good teaching: insights from the work of the Institute of Research on Teaching. *Educational Leadership*, 45, 74-85.

Rosenshine, B.(1980). How time is spent in classrooms. In Denham & Lieberman (Eds.), *Time to Learn*. California Commission for Teacher Preparation and Licensing.

Rosenshine, B. (1986). Synthesis of research on explicit teaching. *Educational Leadership*, 43, 60-69.

Rosenshine, B. & Stevens, R. (1986). Teaching functions. In M. Wittrock (Ed.), *Handbook of Research on Teaching*. New York: Macmillan Publishing Co.

Rowe, M. (1983). Getting chemistry off the killer course list. *Journal of Chemical Education*. 60,11, 954-956.

Rowe, M. (1987). Wait time: slowing down may be a way of speeding up. *American Educator*, Spring, 38-47.

Shuell, T. (1986). Cognitive conceptions of learning. *Review of Educational Research*, 56, 411-436.

Slavin, R. (1988). *Educational Psychology*. Englewood Cliffs, N.J.: Prentice Hall.

Stedman, L. (1995). The new mythology about the status of U.S. schools. *Educational Leadership, 52,* 5, 80-85.

Stevenson, H. (1987). America's math problems. *Educational Leadership,* 45, 4-10.

Stevenson, H. (1993). Why Asian students still outdistance Americans. *Educational Leadership, 50,* 5, 63-65.

Sylwester, R. (1995). *A Celebration of Neurons.* Alexandria, VA: ASCD.

Walberg, H. (1988). Synthesis of research on time and learning. *Educational Leadership,* 45, 76-85.

Walberg, H., Paschal, R. & Weinstein, T. (1985). Homework's powerful effects on learning. *Educational Leadership, 42,* 76-79.

Wang, M., Haertel, G., & Walberg, H. (1993). Toward a knowledge base for school learning. *Review of Educational Research, 63,* 3, 249-294.

Wang, M., Haertel, G., & Walberg, H. (1994). What helps students learn? *Educational Leadership, 51,* 4, 74-79.

Webb, N. (1982). Student interaction and learning in small groups. *Review of Educational Research,* 52, 421-445.

Weiner, B. (1980). *Human Motivation.* New York: Holt, Rinehart & Winston.

Wittrock, M. (1986). Students' thought processes. In M. Wittrock (Ed.), *Handbook of Research on Teaching.* New York: Macmillan Publishing Co.